Campbell's

CREATIVE COOKING
WITH SOUP

Publications International, Ltd.

Fourth edition. First printing.

This edition is an abridged version of *Campbell's Creative Cooking with Soup—Over 19,000 Delicious Mix and Match Recipes.*

©**1988 Campbell Soup Company**

"Campbell's" is a registered trademark of Campbell Soup Company.

This book was prepared by the Publications Center of Campbell Soup Company, Camden, NJ 08103-1799. Betty Cronin, Director of Marketing-Cooking Soups; Julia Malloy and Flora Szatkowski, Editors; Patricia A. Ward and Elaine Gagliardi, Home Economists; William R. Houssell, Photographer; Lynn Wilson/Lee Wilson, Accessories Stylists; Marianne Langan, Food Stylist.

Library of Congress Catalog Card Number: 88-82161

ISBN: 0-88176-813-8

Printed and bound in Yugoslavia

h g f e d c b

Contents

Cooking with Soup... Your Way

Have you ever wished someone would write a cookbook just for you? Someone has, and it's different from other cookbooks you may have used. That's because it's planned for flexibility—to help you with your busy schedule, your family's tastes, your budget, your food supplies, even your creativity.

Each recipe includes a unique chart that shows how you can vary ingredients to suit your needs. For example, when a recipe suggests peas and you don't like peas, you can choose an alternative—possibly corn or spinach. If you're out of cream of mushroom soup, don't panic, the recipe will suggest another soup option. Or, if your budget favors tuna over shrimp, it's your choice.

These variations make every recipe a springboard to as many as 102 different dishes, for a total of more than 10,000 combinations in the book, many with microwave directions. You're sure to find plenty of ways to make everyday meals special and special meals extraordinary.

The secret to making these recipes so versatile is the magic of canned soup. Cream-style soups start a foolproof sauce for dishes requiring one; broth-based soups add a blend of seasonings to foods cooked with liquid.

If you're a beginning cook, you'll appreciate the simplicity of recipes made with soup. If you're more experienced, you'll enjoy the versatility of using soup to create your own new recipes.

You may already know soup as a comforting old-fashioned food, but its adaptability really makes soup very contemporary. It goes into pasta and pizza, quiche and kabobs, tacos and stir-fries, even vegetarian main dishes. Besides these tempting entrées are fresh salads, full-flavored appetizers, hearty soups, even delicious desserts.

You can use these recipes with confidence because they have been carefully tested in Campbell's kitchens. Each variation was tested across the horizontal row of ingredients, but you can experiment with all the other possible combinations. Once you start using the recipes, you'll find your own favorites and you'll see how well they fit into your busy lifestyle. Yes, this book really is written for you!

Recipe Helps

The recipe directions in this book are quite easy to follow, but you may also want to read the points below before preparing the recipes in this book.
- Do not preheat your oven unless the recipe calls for preheating. If your oven manufacturer recommends preheating the broiler, follow those directions.
- Remember that 1 soup can equals about 1¼ cups liquid.
- Measure flour by spooning it lightly into a dry measure, then leveling it off; sifting is not necessary.
- Use dried herbs, unless a fresh herb is specified.
- When light cream or half-and-half is specified, you can use either.
- When green peppers are listed, use bell peppers, not chilies.

How to Use This Book

Each recipe in this book consists of three parts: an ingredient list, a chart and preparation instructions.

Souper Easy Quiche

Ingredient List

4 eggs	½ cup light cream	½ cup **Vegetable**
1 can (10¾ to 11 ounces) condensed **Soup**	1 cup shredded **Cheese**	1 9-inch unbaked piecrust
	Meat	Ground nutmeg

Chart

Soup	Cheese	Meat	Vegetable
Cheddar cheese	sharp Cheddar	½ cup diced cooked ham	drained, cooked chopped broccoli
cream of mushroom	American	6 slices bacon, cooked, drained and crumbled	drained, cooked cut asparagus
cream of chicken	Monterey Jack	½ cup diced cooked chicken	sliced mushrooms
cream of celery	Swiss	½ cup diced cooked turkey	drained, cooked chopped spinach

Preparation Instructions

1. In medium bowl, beat eggs until foamy. Gradually add **Soup** and cream, mixing well.

2. Sprinkle **Cheese, Meat** and **Vegetable** evenly over piecrust. Pour soup mixture over all. Sprinkle with nutmeg.

3. Bake at 350°F. 50 minutes or until center is set. Let stand 10 minutes before serving. Makes 6 servings.

Tip: *To make piecrust: In medium bowl, stir together 1 cup all-purpose flour and ½ teaspoon salt. With pastry blender, cut in ⅓ cup shortening until mixture resembles coarse crumbs. Add 2 to 3 tablespoons cold water, a tablespoon at a time, mixing lightly with fork until pastry holds together. Form into a ball. On lightly floured surface, roll dough to a 13-inch round. Transfer to 9-inch pie plate. Trim edge, leaving ½ inch pastry beyond edge of pie plate. Fold overhang under pastry; pinch to form a high edge. Flute edge.*

Simply read the ingredient list as you would a normal recipe. When you come to an ingredient in **bold** type, refer to the chart. Choose from one of the options listed below the heading. For example, for 1 can condensed **Soup,** look under the heading "Soup" and choose from Cheddar cheese soup, cream of mushroom, cream of chicken and cream of celery.

There are 2 ways to use this chart. You may choose all the items from a single horizontal row as indicated in red or you may skip around as indicated in green.

Once you have made all your selections, just follow the numbered steps.

That's all there is to it! You'll be preparing new recipes in no time.

Microwave Cooking Times

The recipe times given in this book are the *minimum cooking times* needed in 650- to 700-watt ovens. Your oven may consistently require more time than suggested, especially if you have a 400- to 500-watt oven. For the best indicator of cooking time, follow the recipe descriptions of how the food should look when done.

Appetizers

⚜

Appetizer Cheesecake

2 tablespoons butter or margarine
1 cup zwieback crumbs
1 can (10¾ to 11 ounces) condensed
Soup
1 container (15 ounces) ricotta cheese

2 packages (8 ounces each) cream
cheese, softened
Cheese
2 eggs

1 clove garlic, minced
Seasoning
1 cup sour cream
Topper

Soup	Cheese	Seasoning	Topper
cream of celery	1 cup grated Romano	¼ teaspoon dried thyme leaves, crushed	caviar and sieved hard-cooked egg yolk
Cheddar cheese	1½ cups shredded Cheddar	3 tablespoons chopped fresh chives	sliced cucumber, green onion and fresh dill sprigs
tomato	1½ cups shredded Swiss	½ teaspoon dried basil leaves, crushed	tomato roses and green onion tops
cream of chicken	1½ cups shredded Muenster	1 teaspoon curry powder	chutney

1. In small saucepan over medium heat, melt butter; stir in crumbs. Press mixture firmly onto bottom of 9-inch springform pan.

2. In food processor or large bowl, combine **Soup,** ricotta cheese and cream cheese. Process with food processor or beat with electric mixer until smooth. Add **Cheese,** eggs, garlic and **Seasoning.** Beat until smooth. Turn into prepared pan and place in jelly-roll pan.

3. Bake at 325°F. 1½ hours or until puffy and lightly browned. Cool completely in springform pan on wire rack. Cover; refrigerate until serving time, at least 2 hours.

4. Spread sour cream over cake; garnish with **Topper.** Makes 16 appetizer servings.

Sweet and Sour Cocktail Sausages

1 can (10¾ ounces) condensed
tomato soup
¼ cup grape jelly

¼ cup vinegar
Seasoning

1 pound **Sausage**
Garnish

Seasoning	Sausage	Garnish
1 tablespoon prepared mustard	frankfurters, cut into 1-inch pieces	1 can (20 ounces) pineapple chunks, drained
1 tablespoon Worcestershire	kielbasa, cut into bite-sized pieces	2 large green peppers, cut into ¾-inch squares

1. In 2-quart saucepan over medium heat, heat soup, jelly, vinegar and **Seasoning** until jelly melts and mixture is very warm.

2. Meanwhile, place 1 **Sausage** chunk and 1 **Garnish** each on toothpicks or cocktail picks. Add to sauce; heat through, stirring occasionally. Serve hot. Makes about 40 appetizers.

Appetizer Cheesecake

Herbed Seafood Mousse

2 envelopes unflavored gelatin
½ cup water
Seafood

1 can (10¾ ounces) condensed **Soup**
2 eggs, separated
2 tablespoons lemon juice

2 tablespoons finely chopped onion
¼ teaspoon dried **Herb**, crushed
Accompaniment

Seafood	Soup	Herb	Accompaniment
1 can (15½ ounces) salmon, drained	cream of celery	dill weed	rusks (see **Tip** below)
1 bag (10 ounces) frozen shrimp, cooked and drained	cream of chicken	tarragon leaves	crackers
2 cans (about 7 ounces each) tuna, drained	cream of mushroom	basil leaves	fresh vegetables

1. In small saucepan, sprinkle gelatin over water to soften. Over low heat, heat until gelatin is dissolved, stirring constantly.

2. Place **Seafood, Soup,** egg yolks, lemon juice, onion, **Herb** and gelatin mixture in blender container or food processor. Cover; blend or process until smooth.

3. In medium bowl with mixer at high speed, beat egg whites until stiff peaks form. Fold soup mixture into whites. Pour into 6-cup mold. Cover; refrigerate until set, at least 4 hours. Unmold and serve with **Accompaniment.** Makes about 5 cups, 16 appetizer servings.

Tip: To make rusks, cut sliced bread into quarters or cut into fancy shapes with cookie cutters. Arrange in single layer on baking sheet. Bake at 300°F. 10 to 15 minutes until bread is very dry and crisp.

Miniature Quiches

4 eggs
1 can (10¾ to 11 ounces) condensed **Soup**
½ cup half-and-half

¼ teaspoon **Seasoning**
2 tablespoons grated Parmesan cheese
Pastry for 2-crust 9-inch pie

Cheese
¾ cup **Filling**
Ground nutmeg

Soup	Seasoning	Cheese	Filling
cream of celery	dried dill weed, crushed	1 cup shredded Swiss	chopped cooked shrimp
Cheddar cheese	dried oregano leaves, crushed	1 cup shredded Cheddar	diced cooked ham
cream of mushroom	curry powder	1 cup shredded American	drained, cooked chopped broccoli
cream of chicken	dried tarragon leaves, crushed	⅓ cup additional grated Parmesan	drained, cooked chopped asparagus

1. Preheat oven to 425°F. In medium bowl, beat together eggs, **Soup,** half-and-half, **Seasoning** and Parmesan cheese. Set aside.

2. Divide pastry in half. On floured surface, roll out one half of the pastry to ⅛-inch thickness. Cut 9 rounds using 4-inch cookie cutter with scalloped edge. Line 3-inch muffin-pan cups with rounds. Repeat with remaining dough.

3. In small bowl, combine **Cheese** and **Filling.** Divide mixture equally among shells.

4. Place about 2 tablespoons of the soup mixture in each prepared shell. Sprinkle with nutmeg.

5. Bake 20 to 25 minutes until set. Cool in pans on wire racks 5 minutes. Remove from pans and serve. Makes 18 appetizers.

Herbed Seafood Mousse

Mexican-Style Appetizer

1 can (11½ ounces) condensed bean
  with bacon soup
1 package (1¼ ounces) taco seasoning
  mix
¼ teaspoon hot pepper sauce

1 cup sour cream
1 can (4 ounces) chopped green
  chilies, drained
½ cup **Flavoring**

1 cup shredded **Cheese**
½ cup **Topper**
½ cup chopped tomato
Dipper

Flavoring	Cheese	Topper	Dipper
sliced pimento-stuffed olives	longhorn	alfalfa sprouts	tortilla chips
diced cooked ham	Monterey Jack	chopped green pepper	pita bread, torn and toasted
diced avocado	Cheddar	shredded lettuce	celery sticks
diced pepperoni	mozzarella	chopped celery with leaves	sliced jícama (see **Tip** below)

1. In small bowl, combine soup with taco seasoning mix and hot pepper sauce; stir until blended. On large serving plate, spread mixture into a 6-inch round. Spread sides and top of bean mixture with sour cream to cover.

2. Layer chilies, **Flavoring, Cheese, Topper** and tomato over sour cream. Cover; refrigerate until serving time, at least 4 hours. Surround with **Dipper.** Makes 10 appetizer servings.

Tip: *Jícama is a Mexican vegetable that is becoming more readily available in U.S. markets. It is shaped like a turnip, has a brown skin, and may be cooked or eaten raw. To prepare, simply peel jícama and cut into thin slices or strips.*

Pesto Pizza Appetizers

Crust
1 can (10¾ to 11 ounces) condensed
  Soup
2 cloves garlic, minced
½ cup chopped almonds

½ teaspoon dried basil leaves,
  crushed
½ teaspoon dried oregano leaves,
  crushed

1 cup **Vegetable**
¾ cup grated Parmesan cheese
1 cup shredded **Cheese**

Crust	Soup	Vegetable	Cheese
12-inch refrigerated pizza crust	Cheddar cheese	drained, cooked chopped broccoli	mozzarella
2 tubes (7½ ounces each) refrigerated biscuits	cream of chicken	frozen chopped spinach, thawed and drained	longhorn
1 loaf (1 pound) frozen bread dough, thawed	cream of mushroom	chopped fresh parsley	sharp Cheddar

1. Preheat oven to 425°F. Grease 12-inch pizza pan. Place refrigerated crust in pizza pan; pat refrigerated biscuits into pan; or roll out thawed bread dough to fit into pan. Bake **Crust** until top is dry, about 5 minutes for refrigerated crust, about 10 minutes for biscuit or bread dough.

2. Meanwhile, in covered blender or food processor, combine **Soup,** garlic, almonds, basil, oregano, **Vegetable** and Parmesan cheese. Blend or process until smooth.

3. Spread soup mixture over crust. Sprinkle with **Cheese.** Bake 15 minutes more or until pizza is hot and cheese is melted. Cool slightly; cut into squares. Makes 32 appetizer servings.

Tip: *To serve this pizza as a main dish, cut into wedges.*

Mexican-Style Appetizer

Baked Nacho Dip

1 round loaf (about 1 pound) bread
1 can (11 ounces) condensed nacho
  cheese soup/dip

1 package (3 ounces) cream cheese,
  softened
Meat

Vegetable
Garnish

Meat	Vegetable	Garnish
1 can (about 7 ounces) tuna, drained and flaked	½ cup chopped celery	sliced pitted ripe olives
1 cup cooked crab meat, flaked	2 tablespoons sliced green onion	crumbled cooked bacon
1 cup chopped cooked ham	½ cup chopped green pepper	French-fried onion rings
1 cup chopped cooked chicken	½ cup chopped cucumber	chopped tomatoes

1. Preheat oven to 350°F. Slice off top of bread; set aside. Pull out center of loaf, leaving ½-inch shell. Cut top of loaf and center part of bread into 1-inch cubes for dipping; set aside. Place bread shell on baking sheet.

2. In 2-quart saucepan, combine soup, cream cheese, **Meat** and **Vegetable.** Over medium heat, heat through, stirring constantly.

3. Pour soup mixture into bread shell; cover loosely with foil. Bake 20 minutes or until bread is warm. Remove foil; top with **Garnish.** Serve with bread cubes for dipping. Makes about 2½ cups.

Tip: *For a milder flavor, use 8 ounces cream cheese instead of 3 ounces.*

Snappy Cocktail Dip

1 can (10¾ ounces) condensed **Soup**
1 package (8 ounces) cream cheese,
  softened

Seafood
2 tablespoons chopped fresh parsley
2 tablespoons finely chopped onion

Seasoning
Dipper

Soup	Seafood	Seasoning	Dipper
cream of celery	1 can (7¾ ounces) salmon, drained and flaked	¼ teaspoon hot pepper sauce	assorted raw vegetables
cream of mushroom	1 can (6½ ounces) minced clams, drained	2 teaspoons prepared spicy brown mustard	potato chips
cream of chicken	1 can (7 ounces) crab meat, drained and flaked	1 tablespoon lemon juice	melba toast
golden mushroom	1 can (about 7 ounces) tuna, drained and flaked	2 teaspoons prepared horseradish	crackers

1. In medium bowl with mixer at low speed, beat **Soup** into cream cheese just until blended.

2. Stir in **Seafood,** parsley, onion and **Seasoning,** mixing well. Cover; refrigerate until serving time, at least 4 hours. Serve with **Dipper.** Makes about 2¾ cups.

Baked Nacho Dip

Soups

✣

Speedy Potato Chowder

4 slices bacon, diced
½ cup chopped onion

1 can (10¾ ounces) condensed cream
of potato soup
Liquid

1 can (about 8 ounces) **Vegetable**
Meat
2 tablespoons chopped fresh parsley

Liquid	Vegetable	Meat
¾ cup beer plus ¾ cup water	mixed vegetables	1 cup sliced frankfurters
1½ cups milk	whole kernel corn	1 cup diced cooked chicken
1 cup evaporated milk plus ½ cup water	diced carrots	1 can (about 7 ounces) tuna, drained and flaked

1. In 2-quart saucepan over medium heat, cook bacon until crisp. Remove with slotted spoon and drain on paper towels. Pour off all but 1 tablespoon bacon drippings.

2. In hot drippings, cook onion until tender, stirring occasionally. Stir in soup and **Liquid** until well mixed. Add **Vegetable** with its liquid, **Meat,** parsley and reserved bacon. Heat through, stirring occasionally. Makes about 4 cups, 4 servings.

Seafood Chowder

6 slices bacon, diced
1 cup chopped onion
1 can (10¾ ounces) condensed
chicken broth

1 package (5½ ounces) au gratin
potato mix
3½ cups milk

Vegetable
Seasoning
Seafood
Liquid

Vegetable	Seasoning	Seafood	Liquid
1 package (9 ounces) frozen cut green beans, thawed	⅛ teaspoon pepper	1 can (15½ ounces) salmon, drained and broken into chunks	1 can (5 ounces) evaporated milk
1 can (17 ounces) whole kernel corn, drained	⅛ teaspoon lemon-pepper seasoning	2 cans (6½ ounces each) minced clams (do not drain)	⅔ cup light cream
2 cups sliced carrots	⅛ teaspoon paprika	2 cans (about 7 ounces each) tuna, drained	⅓ cup light cream plus ⅓ cup dry white wine
2 cups fresh or frozen peas	¼ teaspoon dried dill weed, crushed	2 cans (4½ ounces each) shrimp, drained	½ cup sour cream

1. In 4-quart Dutch oven over medium heat, cook bacon and onion until bacon is browned and onion is tender, stirring occasionally. Add chicken broth, potato mix with its sauce mix, milk, **Vegetable** and **Seasoning.** Heat to boiling. Reduce heat. Cover; simmer 15 minutes.

2. Stir in **Seafood** and **Liquid.** Cook 5 minutes or until heated through; stir often. Makes about 8 cups, 6 servings.

Speedy Potato Chowder

Chili

1 pound **Meat**
1 cup chopped onion
1 cup chopped green pepper
2 cloves garlic, minced

2 cans (10¾ to 11 ounces each)
condensed **Soup**
1 can (about 15 ounces) **Vegetable**

2 tablespoons chili powder
1 tablespoon vinegar
Garnish

Meat	Soup	Vegetable	Garnish
ground beef	tomato rice	kidney beans	shredded Cheddar cheese
bulk pork sausage	zesty tomato	mixed vegetables	green pepper rings
ground pork	tomato	garbanzo beans	sour cream and sliced green onions

1. In 4-quart Dutch oven over medium heat, cook **Meat,** onion, green pepper and garlic until meat is browned and vegetables are tender, stirring occasionally to break up meat. Pour off fat.

2. Stir in **Soup, Vegetable** with its liquid, chili powder and vinegar. Heat to boiling. Reduce heat to low; simmer, uncovered, 30 minutes, stirring occasionally.

3. Ladle into bowls; top with **Garnish.** Makes about 6½ cups, 6 servings.

To Microwave: In 2-quart microwave-safe casserole, crumble **Meat.** Add onion, green pepper and garlic; cover. Microwave on HIGH 7 to 9 minutes until meat is nearly done, stirring occasionally. Pour off fat. Stir in **Soup, Vegetable** with its liquid, chili powder and vinegar; cover. Microwave on HIGH 12 to 15 minutes until heated through, stirring occasionally. Ladle into bowls; top with **Garnish.**

Baked Sausage-Bean Soup

2 tablespoons vegetable oil
1 cup chopped onion
1 clove garlic, minced
1 can (10½ to 10¾ ounces)
condensed **Soup**

1 can (about 16 ounces) **Beans**
½ cup diced **Sausage**
1 can (4 ounces) chopped green chilies, drained

1 can (about 16 ounces) tomatoes, cut up
½ cup water
1½ cups cubed French bread
1 cup shredded **Cheese**

Soup	Beans	Sausage	Cheese
minestrone	garbanzo beans	kielbasa	colby
vegetable	pork and beans in tomato sauce	frankfurters	Provolone
tomato	green beans	pepperoni	mozzarella

1. In 3-quart saucepan over medium heat, in hot oil, cook onion and garlic until tender, stirring occasionally.

2. Stir in **Soup, Beans** with their liquid, **Sausage,** chilies, tomatoes with their liquid and water. Heat to boiling. Reduce heat to low. Cover; simmer 10 minutes to blend flavors. Preheat oven to 450°F.

3. Ladle soup into six 10-ounce ovenproof bowls; place on jelly-roll pan. Sprinkle with bread and **Cheese.**

4. Bake 10 minutes until top is golden brown and cheese is melted. Makes about 6 cups, 6 servings.

Chili

Pasta and Bean Soup

Meat
½ cup chopped onion
½ cup chopped celery
½ cup shredded carrot

1 clove garlic, minced
1 can (10½ ounces) condensed **Soup**
1 soup can water
1 can (about 19 ounces) white kidney beans

½ teaspoon dried **Herb,** crushed
1 bay leaf
⅛ teaspoon pepper
½ cup uncooked **Pasta**

Meat	Soup	Herb	Pasta
½ cup diced cooked ham plus 2 tablespoons vegetable oil	vegetable	thyme leaves	small shell macaroni
4 slices bacon, diced	minestrone	oregano leaves	elbow macaroni

1. In 4-quart Dutch oven over medium heat, cook **Meat** until lightly browned, stirring occasionally. Add onion, celery, carrot and garlic; cook until vegetables are tender, stirring occasionally.

2. Stir in **Soup,** water, beans with their liquid, **Herb,** bay leaf and pepper. Heat to boiling. Reduce heat to low. Cover; simmer 15 minutes.

3. Stir in **Pasta;** cook about 12 minutes more or until pasta is tender. Discard bay leaf. Makes about 5 cups, 4 servings.

Hearty Bean Soup

1 cup dry **Beans**
8½ cups water, divided
¼ pound smoked pork butt or ham
1 cup chopped onion
½ cup chopped green pepper

1 clove garlic, minced
Seasoning
¼ teaspoon pepper
1 bay leaf

1 can (10¾ ounces) condensed cream of potato soup
Vegetable 1
Vegetable 2
½ cup chopped green onions

Beans	Seasoning	Vegetable 1	Vegetable 2
navy beans	½ teaspoon dried thyme leaves, crushed	2 cups coarsely chopped cabbage	1 cup sliced carrots
red kidney beans	2 tablespoons chili powder	2 cups diced tomatoes	1 cup whole kernel corn
garbanzo beans	1 tablespoon curry powder	1 cup cut green beans	1 small butternut squash, peeled and cubed
pinto beans	½ teaspoon ground cumin	2 cups sliced zucchini	1 cup sliced okra

1. In 4-quart Dutch oven over high heat, heat **Beans** and 5 cups of the water to boiling. Boil, uncovered, 2 minutes. Remove from heat and let stand, covered, 1 hour. Drain.

2. Add remaining 3½ cups water, pork, onion, green pepper, garlic, **Seasoning,** pepper and bay leaf. Over high heat, heat to boiling; reduce heat to low. Cover; simmer 1½ hours.

3. Remove pork from soup. Cool until easy to handle. Dice pork and return to soup.

4. Add potato soup, **Vegetable 1** and **Vegetable 2.** Cover; simmer 25 minutes more or until vegetables are tender. Add water, if needed, to make desired consistency. Discard bay leaf. Just before serving, stir in green onions. Makes about 5 cups, 4 servings.

Pasta and Bean Soup

Five-Minute Vegetable Soup

1 can (10½ to 10¾ ounces)
condensed **Soup**
1 can (14½ ounces) stewed tomatoes

1 can (about 8 ounces) whole kernel
corn, drained
1 cup **Protein**

1 cup **Vegetable**
Seasoning
Chopped fresh parsley for garnish

Soup	Protein	Vegetable	Seasoning
chicken broth	cubed cooked chicken	French-cut green beans	¼ teaspoon dried rosemary leaves, crushed
French onion	cooked beef cut into strips	cut asparagus	½ teaspoon dried thyme leaves, crushed
beef broth	thinly sliced kielbasa	shredded cabbage	⅛ teaspoon pepper
won ton	cubed tofu	chopped fresh spinach	1 clove garlic, minced

1. In 3-quart saucepan, combine **Soup**, tomatoes, corn, **Protein**, **Vegetable** and **Seasoning**. Over high heat, heat to boiling.

2. Reduce heat to low; simmer, uncovered, 5 minutes. Garnish with parsley. Makes about 6 cups, 5 servings.

Tip: *To make a more substantial soup, mound ½ cup hot cooked rice in each bowl before ladling soup over.*

Oriental-Style Soup

1 egg white
½ pound **Meat**
¼ cup finely chopped water
chestnuts

1 tablespoon cornstarch
1 teaspoon soy sauce
¼ teaspoon minced fresh ginger
Vegetable 1

2 cans (10¾ ounces each) condensed
chicken broth
1 soup can water
Vegetable 2
Garnish

Meat	Vegetable 1	Vegetable 2	Garnish
ground pork	1 cup sliced celery	½ cup peas	chopped green onions
raw chicken, finely chopped	1 cup carrots cut into julienne strips	½ cup sliced water chestnuts	sliced radishes
medium shrimp, shelled, deveined and finely chopped	1 ounce bean threads (available in Oriental markets)	½ cup snow peas	cilantro sprigs

1. In medium bowl with fork, beat egg white until foamy. Add **Meat,** water chestnuts, cornstarch, soy sauce and ginger; mix well.

2. In 4-quart saucepan over high heat, heat 2 quarts water to boiling. Drop meat mixture by teaspoonfuls into water. Reduce heat; simmer 2 to 5 minutes until meat is done and balls rise to surface. Remove balls with slotted spoon; set aside. Discard water.

3. If using bean threads for **Vegetable 1,** cut threads into 2-inch lengths. In bowl, add enough hot water to bean threads to cover; let stand 15 minutes. Drain. (If using other variations, proceed to Step 4.)

4. In same saucepan over high heat, heat chicken broth and 1 soup can water to boiling. Add **Vegetable 1;** reduce heat. Simmer 5 minutes. Add **Vegetable 2;** simmer 2 minutes more.

5. Add balls to broth; heat through. Ladle into bowls; top with **Garnish.** Makes about 6 cups, 6 servings.

Tip: *Chop chicken or shrimp in food processor for best results.*

Five-Minute Vegetable Soup

Creamy Vegetable Bisque

2 tablespoons butter or margarine
1 cup **Vegetable**
1 cup sliced celery

½ cup chopped onion
1 can (10¾ ounces) condensed **Soup**
1 soup can milk

Seasoning
Garnish

Vegetable	Soup	Seasoning	Garnish
carrots cut into 1-inch julienne strips	cream of mushroom	⅛ teaspoon pepper	grated Romano cheese
broccoli flowerets cut into bite-sized pieces	cream of asparagus	½ teaspoon ground nutmeg	toasted slivered almonds
cauliflowerets cut into bite-sized pieces	creamy chicken mushroom	¼ teaspoon dry mustard	chopped fresh parsley
cut asparagus	cream of celery	¼ teaspoon dried thyme leaves, crushed	lemon slices

1. In 2-quart saucepan over medium heat, in hot butter, cook **Vegetable**, celery and onion 5 to 10 minutes until vegetables are tender-crisp, stirring frequently.

2. Stir in **Soup,** milk and **Seasoning.** Heat through. Ladle into bowls; top with **Garnish.** Makes about 3½ cups, 4 servings.

Extra-Good Cream Soup

2 tablespoons butter or margarine
½ cup chopped onion
Vegetable

½ teaspoon dried **Herb,** crushed
1 can (10¾ ounces) condensed **Soup**
½ cup light cream

¾ cup milk
Garnish

Vegetable	Herb	Soup	Garnish
1 medium tomato, diced	tarragon leaves	tomato	grated Parmesan cheese
1 cup sliced mushrooms	thyme leaves	cream of mushroom	chopped fresh parsley
1 cup fresh or frozen cut asparagus	dill weed	cream of asparagus	oyster crackers
1 cup sliced celery	marjoram leaves	cream of celery	melba toast

1. In 2-quart saucepan over medium heat, in hot butter, cook onion, **Vegetable** and **Herb** until vegetables are tender, stirring occasionally.

2. Stir in **Soup,** cream and milk. Heat through, stirring occasionally. Ladle into bowls; serve with **Garnish.** Makes about 3½ cups, 4 servings.

To Microwave: In 2-quart microwave-safe casserole, combine butter, onion, **Vegetable** and **Herb;** cover. Microwave on HIGH 7 to 9 minutes until vegetables are tender, stirring once. Stir in **Soup,** cream and milk; cover. Microwave on HIGH 5 to 7 minutes until heated through, stirring occasionally. Ladle into bowls; serve with **Garnish.**

Creamy Vegetable Bisque

Clear Vegetable Soup

| 1 can (10¾ ounces) condensed chicken broth | 1 soup can water Vegetable | Starch Garnish |

Vegetable	Starch	Garnish
½ cup sliced carrot plus ½ cup sliced celery	¼ cup rotelle or other macaroni	1 teaspoon chopped fresh parsley
½ cup chopped tomato plus ½ cup chopped green onions	2 tablespoons regular rice, uncooked	1 tablespoon grated Parmesan cheese
1 cup frozen mixed vegetables	¼ cup pearled barley	1 teaspoon chopped fresh chives
½ cup sliced mushrooms plus ½ cup sliced leek	2 tablespoons brown rice, uncooked	2 slices bacon, cooked, drained and crumbled

1. In 2-quart saucepan over high heat, heat chicken broth, water and **Vegetable** to boiling. Add **Starch.** Reduce heat to low. Cover; simmer until starch is done, about 20 minutes for macaroni or regular rice, about 40 minutes for barley or brown rice.

2. Ladle soup into bowls; top with **Garnish**. Makes about 3 cups, 3 servings.

Onion Soup au Gratin

| 2 tablespoons vegetable oil 1 tablespoon butter or margarine 1 pound onions, sliced (4 cups) ¼ teaspoon sugar | 2 cans (10½ to 10¾ ounces each) condensed **Soup** 2 soup cans water | **Bread** 2 cups shredded **Cheese** ¼ cup grated Parmesan cheese |

Soup	Bread	Cheese
beef broth	6 slices French bread, toasted	Swiss
beef noodle	2 cups croutons	Gruyère
chicken broth	6 slices rye bread, toasted	Cheddar
chicken noodle	3 croissants, split horizontally and toasted	mozzarella

1. In covered 3-quart saucepan over low heat, in hot oil and butter, cook onions 15 minutes or until tender, stirring occasionally.

2. Uncover; stir in sugar. Over medium heat, cook 30 minutes more or until onions are golden, stirring frequently.

3. Add **Soup** and water. Heat to boiling; reduce heat to low. Cover; simmer 25 minutes. Preheat oven to 350°F.

4. Ladle soup into six 12-ounce ovenproof bowls; place bowls on jelly-roll pan. Place **Bread** in each bowl and top each with **Cheese** and Parmesan. Bake 20 minutes or until cheese is melted and top is browned. Makes about 6½ cups, 6 servings.

Tip: *If you wish, stir in ½ cup dry white wine while soup is simmering.*

Clear Vegetable Soup

Main Dishes

✤

Stir-Fried Beef and Vegetables

½ pound boneless beef sirloin steak
1 can (10½ to 10¾ ounces)
condensed **Soup**
1 tablespoon cornstarch

1 tablespoon soy sauce
3 tablespoons vegetable oil, divided
1 clove garlic, minced
4 green onions, cut into 1-inch pieces

1 cup **Vegetable 1**
Vegetable 2
Accompaniment

Soup	Vegetable 1	Vegetable 2	Accompaniment
beef broth	fresh or frozen cut broccoli	1 can (8 ounces) sliced bamboo shoots, drained	shredded lettuce
chicken with rice	sliced celery	1 cup fresh or canned bean sprouts	chow mein noodles
chicken broth	fresh or frozen cut asparagus	1 can (8 ounces) sliced water chestnuts, drained	hot cooked noodles

1. Freeze steak 1 hour to make slicing easier. Trim and discard excess fat from steak. Cut steak into very thin slices; set aside. In small bowl, combine **Soup,** cornstarch and soy sauce; stir to blend. Set aside.

2. In 10-inch skillet or wok over medium-high heat, in 2 tablespoons hot oil, stir-fry beef strips and garlic until meat is browned; remove from skillet.

3. Add remaining 1 tablespoon oil to skillet. Add green onions and **Vegetable 1;** stir-fry 1 minute. Add **Vegetable 2;** stir-fry 30 seconds more.

4. Return beef to skillet. Stir soup mixture; stir into skillet. Heat to boiling; cook 1 minute more. Spoon over **Accompaniment.** Makes about 2½ cups, 2 servings.

Ribs and Lentils

1 tablespoon vegetable oil
2 pounds **Meat**
1 can (10½ ounces) condensed
French onion soup
1 cup sliced celery and celery leaves

2 cloves garlic, minced
¼ teaspoon pepper
½ teaspoon dried **Herb**, crushed
1 pound dry lentils, rinsed

1 can (10¾ to 11 ounces) condensed
Soup
1 cup sliced carrots
4 cups water
Garnish

Meat	Herb	Soup	Garnish
beef short ribs, cut into 1-rib pieces	marjoram leaves	tomato	chopped fresh parsley
pork spareribs, cut into 2-rib pieces	basil leaves	tomato rice	chopped tomatoes

1. In 6-quart Dutch oven over medium-high heat, in hot oil, cook **Meat** until browned on all sides. Pour off fat.

2. Add French onion soup, celery, garlic, pepper and **Herb.** Heat to boiling; reduce heat to low. Cover; simmer 1 hour.

3. Add lentils, **Soup,** carrots and water. Cover; simmer 1 hour or until meat and lentils are tender. Sprinkle with **Garnish.** Makes about 11 cups, 8 servings.

Stir-Fried Beef and Vegetables

Beef Stew

2 pounds beef for stew, cut into
1-inch cubes
¼ cup all-purpose flour
4 tablespoons **Fat,** divided
2 medium onions, sliced

2 cloves garlic, minced
1 teaspoon dried **Herb,** crushed
1 bay leaf
1 can (10½ to 10¾ ounces)
condensed **Soup**

½ cup water
Vegetable
2 medium carrots, cut into 2- by
½-inch strips
1 cup fresh or frozen cut green beans

Fat	Herb	Soup	Vegetable
shortening	thyme leaves	beefy mushroom	3 medium potatoes, peeled and cubed
salad oil	marjoram leaves	beef broth	1 medium turnip, peeled and cubed
butter or margarine	rosemary leaves	French onion	3 medium parsnips, peeled and cut into 1-inch chunks
bacon drippings	basil leaves	consommé	3 medium sweet potatoes, peeled and cubed

1. Coat beef cubes with flour; reserve remaining flour.

2. In 4-quart Dutch oven over medium-high heat, in 2 table-spoons hot **Fat,** cook beef, a few pieces at a time, until browned on all sides. Remove beef as it browns. Reduce heat to medium.

3. Add remaining 2 tablespoons **Fat** to Dutch oven. In hot fat, cook onions, garlic, **Herb** and bay leaf until onions are tender, stirring occasionally. Stir in reserved flour. Gradually add **Soup** and water; heat to boiling. Return meat to pan. Reduce heat to low. Cover; simmer 1 hour, stirring occasionally.

4. Add **Vegetable,** carrots and green beans. Cover; simmer 25 minutes or until vegetables are tender. Discard bay leaf. Makes about 6 cups, 8 servings.

Easy Pot Roast

Fat
3½-pound beef chuck pot roast

1 can (10¾ ounces) condensed **Soup**
1 teaspoon dried **Herb,** crushed

2 tablespoons all-purpose flour
¼ cup **Liquid**

Fat	Soup	Herb	Liquid
2 tablespoons shortening	cream of mushroom	thyme leaves	heavy cream
2 tablespoons vegetable oil	cream of celery	rosemary leaves	dry white wine
non-stick cooking spray	golden mushroom	marjoram leaves	water

1. In 6-quart Dutch oven over medium-high heat, in hot **Fat,** brown beef on all sides. Pour off fat.

2. Stir in **Soup** and **Herb.** Reduce heat to low. Cover; simmer 2½ to 3 hours until tender, stirring occasionally. Add water during cooking, if necessary.

3. Remove beef to platter; keep warm. In screw-top jar, shake together flour and **Liquid** until smooth; stir into pan drippings. Over high heat, heat to boiling, stirring constantly. Cook 1 minute more.

4. Cut meat into thin slices. Serve gravy with meat. Makes 8 servings.

Beef Stew

Teriyaki Beef Kabobs

1 can (10½ to 10¾ ounces)
condensed **Soup**
¼ cup dry sherry
¼ cup soy sauce
1 large clove garlic, minced

Seasoning
1 tablespoon **Sweetener**
1½ pounds boneless beef sirloin
steak, cut 1 inch thick
1 medium green pepper, cut into
1-inch squares

1 pound small whole onions, cooked
and drained
½ cup pineapple chunks
Accompaniment

Soup	Seasoning	Sweetener	Accompaniment
French onion	¼ cup sliced green onions	honey	hot cooked rice
beef broth	¼ cup finely chopped onion	brown sugar	hot cooked wild rice
tomato	½ teaspoon ground ginger	sugar	hot cooked bulgur wheat

1. To make marinade: In medium bowl, combine **Soup**, sherry, soy sauce, garlic, **Seasoning** and **Sweetener**.

2. Cut beef into 1-inch cubes; add to marinade. Cover; refrigerate 3 hours or overnight, stirring once or twice.

3. Drain meat, reserving marinade. Thread beef cubes, green pepper, onions and pineapple chunks on six 12-inch skewers.

4. On rack in broiler pan, broil 6 inches from heat 10 minutes or until meat is cooked to desired doneness, turning and brushing often with marinade. Serve with **Accompaniment**. Makes 6 servings.

Tip: Assemble skewers before marinating. Place in shallow dish; pour marinade over skewers. Cover; refrigerate 3 hours or overnight, turning occasionally.

Barbecued Beef Sandwiches

1 pound ground beef
½ cup chopped onion
½ cup chopped green pepper
1 clove garlic, minced

1 can (10½ to 11¼ ounces)
condensed **Soup**
1 can (10¾ ounces) condensed
tomato soup

2 tablespoons vinegar
Seasoning
¼ teaspoon pepper
Bread, split and toasted

Soup	Seasoning	Bread
chili beef plus ¼ cup water	1 teaspoon dry mustard	8 hamburger buns
golden mushroom	¼ teaspoon hot pepper sauce	8 hard rolls
vegetarian vegetable	1 teaspoon chili powder	8 frankfurter buns

1. In 10-inch skillet over medium heat, cook ground beef, onion, green pepper and garlic until meat is browned and vegetables are tender, stirring often to break up meat. Pour off fat.

2. Stir in **Soup**, tomato soup, vinegar, **Seasoning** and pepper. Heat to boiling, stirring occasionally. Reduce heat to low. Simmer, uncovered, 20 minutes or until desired consistency. Serve in or over **Bread,** using about ⅓ cup per serving. Makes 8 servings.

To Microwave: In 2-quart microwave-safe casserole, crumble beef. Add onion, green pepper and garlic; cover. Microwave on HIGH 6 to 8 minutes until meat is browned and vegetables are tender, stirring occasionally. Pour off fat. Stir in **Soup**, tomato soup, vinegar, **Seasoning** and pepper; cover. Microwave on HIGH 7 to 9 minutes until boiling, stirring occasionally. Serve as in Step 2.

Teriyaki Beef Kabobs

Meat Loaf Supreme

1 can (10¾ ounces) condensed **Soup,** divided
1½ pounds ground beef
½ cup chopped onion

½ cup fine dry bread crumbs
1 egg
Topper
⅓ cup milk

1 teaspoon honey
Seasoning
Flavoring

Soup	Topper	Seasoning	Flavoring
cream of mushroom	1 package (8 ounces) refrigerated crescent rolls	¼ teaspoon dried dill weed, crushed	2 teaspoons Dijon-style mustard
tomato	pastry for one 9-inch piecrust	½ teaspoon curry powder	1 tablespoon creamy peanut butter
cream of celery	½ sheet frozen puff pastry, thawed	½ teaspoon ground ginger	1 teaspoon soy sauce plus 1 teaspoon dry sherry
golden mushroom	2 cups seasoned mashed potatoes	¼ teaspoon dried thyme leaves, crushed	1 teaspoon Worcestershire

1. In large bowl, thoroughly mix ½ cup of the **Soup,** beef, onion, crumbs and egg. In 12- by 8-inch baking dish, firmly shape mixture into 8- by 4-inch loaf. Bake at 350°F. 1 hour. Remove meat loaf from oven; pour off fat.

2. *For crescent rolls,* unroll and separate dough into triangles. Place triangles crosswise over top and down sides of meat loaf, overlapping triangles. Bake 15 minutes or until browned.

For piecrust or puff pastry, turn oven to 400°F. On lightly floured surface, roll out pastry and trim to 10- by 8-inch rectangle. Lay pastry over meat loaf, tucking edges under loaf to hold in place. Bake 15 minutes or until browned.

For mashed potatoes, turn oven to 450°F. Prepare mashed potatoes; spread over meat loaf. Bake 15 minutes or until potatoes just begin to brown.

3. Meanwhile, to prepare sauce: In 1-quart saucepan, stir together remaining **Soup,** milk, honey, **Seasoning** and **Flavoring.** Over medium heat, heat to boiling, stirring constantly. Serve with meat loaf. Makes 6 servings.

Miniature Meat Loaves

1½ pounds ground beef
1 can (10½ ounces) condensed **Soup**
Crumbs

½ cup chopped onion
⅓ cup **Vegetable**
2 tablespoons chopped fresh parsley

Dried **Herb,** crushed
¼ teaspoon pepper

Soup	Crumbs	Vegetable	Herb
vegetarian vegetable	2 cups soft bread crumbs	chopped green pepper	1 teaspoon oregano leaves
minestrone	1 cup fine dry bread crumbs	shredded carrot	½ teaspoon thyme leaves

1. In large bowl, thoroughly mix all ingredients. Firmly shape mixture into 6 small meat loaves. Place loaves in 15- by 10-inch jelly-roll pan.

2. Bake at 375°F. 40 minutes or until done. Makes 6 servings.

To Microwave: Use ingredients as above but substitute 1 cup fine dry bread crumbs for **Crumbs** in all variations. Combine all ingredients as directed in Step 1. Firmly press mixture into six 6-ounce microwave-safe custard cups. Arrange custard cups in a ring in microwave oven. Microwave on HIGH 15 to 18 minutes until firm to the touch, rearranging once. Let stand 5 to 7 minutes.

Meat Loaf Supreme

Best-Ever Meat Loaf

1 can (10¾ to 11 ounces) condensed **Soup,** divided
Meat

Crumbs
1 egg, beaten
⅓ cup finely chopped onion

Seasoning
⅓ cup water

Soup	Meat	Crumbs	Seasoning
golden mushroom	2 pounds ground beef	½ cup fine dry bread crumbs	1 tablespoon Worcestershire
cream of mushroom	2 pounds meat loaf mix (beef, pork, veal)	½ cup quick-cooking oats	1 tablespoon soy sauce
Cheddar cheese	1½ pounds ground beef plus ½ pound Italian sausage, casings removed	½ cup finely crushed saltine crackers	¼ cup chopped pimento-stuffed olives

1. In large bowl, thoroughly mix ½ cup of the **Soup, Meat, Crumbs,** egg, onion and **Seasoning.** In 12- by 8-inch baking pan, firmly shape meat into 8- by 4-inch loaf.

2. Bake at 350°F. 1¼ hours or until done. Remove meat loaf to platter; keep warm.

3. Pour off all but 3 tablespoons drippings from pan. Stir remaining **Soup** and water into drippings in pan, scraping up brown bits from bottom. Over medium heat, heat soup mixture until hot, stirring constantly. Serve gravy with meat loaf. Makes 8 servings.

Tip: *If you use a glass baking dish for your meat loaf, prepare as above in Steps 1 and 2. Pour 3 tablespoons drippings into a small saucepan; discard remaining drippings. Stir remaining **Soup** and water into saucepan. Over medium heat, heat soup mixture until hot, stirring constantly. Serve as above.*

Spread-a-Burger

1 can (10¾ to 11 ounces) condensed **Soup**
1½ pounds **Meat**

Seasoning
⅓ cup chopped onion
⅛ teaspoon pepper

8 long hard rolls, split
2 cups shredded **Cheese**

Soup	Meat	Seasoning	Cheese
Cheddar cheese	bulk pork sausage	½ teaspoon celery seed	mozzarella
tomato	ground beef	1 tablespoon Worcestershire	Cheddar
cream of mushroom	ground pork	1 tablespoon prepared horseradish	Swiss
golden mushroom	ground lamb	1 tablespoon prepared mustard	American

1. In large bowl, blend **Soup, Meat, Seasoning,** onion and pepper until thoroughly mixed. Spread ¼ cup of the meat mixture evenly on each roll half, spreading to cover edges.

2. Place rolls, meat side up, on baking sheet. Broil 4 to 6 inches from heat 7 to 8 minutes until meat is done.

3. Sprinkle rolls with **Cheese;** broil until cheese melts. Makes 8 servings.

Savory Meatballs

1 can (10¾ ounces) condensed **Soup**
½ cup water
2 tablespoons chopped fresh parsley

1 pound ground beef
Crumbs
¼ cup **Vegetable**

1 egg, beaten
½ teaspoon dried **Herb,** crushed
1 tablespoon vegetable oil

Soup	Crumbs	Vegetable	Herb
beefy mushroom	¼ cup fine dry bread crumbs	finely chopped onion	thyme leaves
cream of mushroom	¼ cup finely crushed saltine crackers	shredded carrot	marjoram leaves
cream of celery	½ cup soft bread crumbs	finely chopped green pepper	basil leaves
golden mushroom	¼ cup finely crushed corn flakes	finely chopped celery	dill weed

1. In small bowl, combine **Soup,** water and parsley; set aside.

2. In medium bowl, combine ground beef, **Crumbs, Vegetable,** egg and **Herb.** Mix lightly, but well. Shape into 16 meatballs.

3. In 10-inch skillet over medium heat, in hot oil, cook meatballs, half at a time, until browned on all sides. Pour off fat. Stir soup mixture into skillet. Reduce heat to low. Cover; simmer 20 minutes. Makes 4 servings.

To Microwave: Use ingredients as above but omit oil. Prepare as above in Steps 1 and 2. In 12- by 8-inch microwave-safe baking dish, place meatballs; cover. Microwave on HIGH 4 to 5 minutes until almost done, turning over and rearranging meatballs once. Pour off fat. Stir soup mixture into dish; cover. Microwave on HIGH 4 to 6 minutes until heated through, stirring once.

Rice Pizza

3 cups cooked rice (about 1 cup uncooked)
2 cups shredded **Cheese,** divided
2 eggs, beaten

½ pound bulk pork sausage
1 can (10¾ ounces) condensed tomato soup
¼ teaspoon **Seasoning**

Vegetable
Topper
¼ cup grated Romano cheese

Cheese	Seasoning	Vegetable	Topper
sharp Cheddar	dried oregano leaves, crushed	1 medium zucchini, sliced	¼ cup sliced pimento-stuffed olives
mozzarella	dried marjoram leaves, crushed	1 cup sliced mushrooms	¼ cup chopped green pepper
Monterey Jack	chili powder	1 cup fresh or frozen whole kernel corn	2 tablespoons finely chopped drained green chilies
colby	Italian seasoning, crushed	1 medium onion, sliced and separated into rings	1 can (2 ounces) anchovy fillets, drained

1. Grease 12-inch pizza pan. Preheat oven to 450°F.

2. In medium bowl, combine rice, ¾ cup of the **Cheese** and eggs; mix well. Pat mixture evenly onto prepared pizza pan, building up ½-inch rim. Bake 15 minutes or until crust is set.

3. Meanwhile, in 10-inch skillet over medium heat, cook sausage until browned, stirring to break up meat. Remove sausage from pan; drain on paper towels.

4. In small bowl, stir together soup and **Seasoning.** Spread over baked crust. Arrange **Vegetable,** cooked sausage, **Topper,** remaining 1¼ cups **Cheese** and Romano cheese over soup.

5. Bake 15 minutes or until crust is golden brown and cheese is melted. Makes 6 servings.

Sausage and Peppers

1 pound Italian sausage, cut into
2-inch chunks
2 tablespoons water
2 large green peppers, cut into
½-inch-wide strips

1 medium onion, sliced and separated
into rings
2 cloves garlic, minced
1 can (10¾ to 11 ounces) condensed
Soup

½ cup water
½ teaspoon dried **Herb,** crushed
Accompaniment

Soup	Herb	Accompaniment
zesty tomato	basil leaves	polenta (see **Tip** below)
tomato	marjoram leaves	hot cooked spaghetti

1. In 10-inch covered skillet over medium heat, cook sausage and 2 tablespoons water 5 minutes. Uncover; cook until sausages are browned on all sides.

2. Add green peppers, onion and garlic; cook until vegetables are tender, stirring frequently. Pour off fat.

3. Stir in **Soup,** ½ cup water and **Herb;** reduce heat to low.

Cover; simmer 10 minutes. Serve with **Accompaniment.** Makes 4 servings.

Tip: *To prepare polenta: In heavy 4-quart saucepan, heat 4 cups water and 1 teaspoon salt to boiling. With wire whisk, gradually stir in 1 cup cornmeal. Reduce heat to low. Simmer 20 to 25 minutes, stirring often. Pour into buttered 9-inch pie plate. Let stand 10 minutes; cut into wedges.*

Meat-Vegetable Packets

1 can (10¾ to 11 ounces) condensed
Soup
1 cup **Vegetable**

½ teaspoon dried **Herb,** crushed
4 medium carrots, thinly sliced
4 medium potatoes, thinly sliced

1 medium onion, sliced
¼ teaspoon pepper
Meat

Soup	Vegetable	Herb	Meat
golden mushroom	fresh or frozen peas	thyme leaves	4 pork chops, each cut ½ inch thick
cream of chicken	sliced mushrooms	rosemary leaves	2 pounds chicken parts
Cheddar cheese	fresh or frozen cut green beans	dill weed	4 ground beef patties (¼ pound each)
cream of celery	sliced zucchini	marjoram leaves	4 veal chops, each cut ½ inch thick

1. Tear off four 12-inch lengths of heavy foil.

2. In medium bowl, stir together **Soup, Vegetable, Herb,** carrots, potatoes, onion and pepper. Divide mixture onto foil; top each with ¼ of the **Meat.** Fold foil around food to make a tight package.

3. Bake at 350°F. 1¼ hours or until meat and vegetables are tender. Makes 4 servings.

Tip: *Packets can be cooked on charcoal or gas grill over medium coals.*

Sausage and Peppers

Sausage-Vegetable Rolls

½ pound bulk pork sausage
1 cup chopped onion
1 cup **Vegetable**

1 can (10¾ to 11 ounces) condensed
Soup
1 loaf (1 pound) frozen bread dough,
thawed

½ cup **Cheese**
1 egg, beaten
1 tablespoon **Topping**

Vegetable	Soup	Cheese	Topping
frozen chopped broccoli, thawed and drained	golden mushroom	grated Romano	sesame seed
sauerkraut, rinsed and drained	cream of celery	shredded Swiss	wheat germ
frozen chopped spinach, thawed and drained	Cheddar cheese	shredded Cheddar	poppy seed

1. Preheat oven to 350°F. Grease large baking sheet.

2. In 10-inch skillet over medium heat, cook sausage until it begins to brown, stirring to break up meat. Add onion and **Vegetable;** cook about 5 minutes until meat is browned and vegetables are tender, stirring occasionally. Pour off fat. Stir in **Soup.** Cool.

3. Divide thawed dough into 6 equal parts. On floured surface, roll out 1 part to a 6-inch round. Place about ½ cup of the sausage mixture on dough, spreading to within 1 inch of edges. Sprinkle with 1 generous tablespoon of the **Cheese.** Fold over to form a half circle. Pinch edges to seal. Place on prepared baking sheet. Repeat with remaining dough.

4. Brush rolls with egg; sprinkle with **Topping.** Bake 25 minutes or until golden brown. Let stand 10 minutes. Serve warm. Makes 6 servings.

Stuffed Cabbage Leaves

1 pound **Meat**
½ cup chopped onion
1 can (10½ ounces) condensed beef
broth
½ cup **Grain,** uncooked

½ teaspoon grated lemon peel
½ cup **Fruit**
¼ cup chopped walnuts
¼ cup chopped fresh parsley
½ teaspoon dried mint leaves
(optional)

1 medium head cabbage
1 can (10¾ to 11 ounces) condensed
Soup
1 tablespoon lemon juice
¼ teaspoon ground cinnamon

Meat	Grain	Fruit	Soup
ground pork	bulgur wheat	chopped apple	tomato
ground beef	regular rice	golden raisins	tomato rice

1. In 10-inch skillet over medium heat, cook **Meat** and onion until meat is well browned, stirring occasionally to break up meat. Pour off fat.

2. Add beef broth, **Grain** and lemon peel. Heat to boiling. Reduce heat to low. Cover; simmer 20 to 25 minutes until grain is tender. Add a little water during cooking if mixture becomes dry. Remove from heat. Stir in **Fruit,** walnuts, parsley and mint.

3. Meanwhile, in 4-quart saucepan over high heat, heat about 6 cups water to boiling. Add whole head of cabbage to boiling water. Reduce heat to low. Cover; simmer 1 to 2 minutes or until outer leaves are softened. Remove cabbage from water. Carefully remove 6 outer leaves. Reserve remaining cabbage for another use.

4. Drain cabbage leaves on paper towels. Lay leaves flat on cutting board and cut out any tough stems. Spoon about ¾ cup of the meat filling into center of one leaf. Fold in sides, then roll up from stem end to form a bundle. Repeat with remaining leaves and filling.

5. In medium bowl, stir together **Soup,** lemon juice and cinnamon. Pour ½ of the soup mixture into 12- by 8-inch baking dish. Place cabbage rolls, seam side down, in prepared dish. Pour remaining soup mixture over all. Cover with foil. Bake at 350°F. 35 minutes or until heated through. Makes 6 servings.

Sausage-Vegetable Rolls

Lasagna Roll-Ups

1 pound **Meat**
1 cup chopped onion
2 cloves garlic, minced
1 tablespoon dried **Herb**, crushed
1 can (10¾ ounces) condensed
tomato soup

1 cup water
1 can (6 ounces) tomato paste
1½ pounds ricotta cheese
1 cup shredded **Cheese 1**
2 tablespoons chopped fresh parsley

¼ teaspoon ground nutmeg
8 lasagna noodles, cooked and
drained
¼ cup grated **Cheese 2**

Meat	Herb	Cheese 1	Cheese 2
Italian sausage, casings removed	oregano leaves	mozzarella	Parmesan
ground pork	basil leaves	longhorn	Romano
ground beef	marjoram leaves	Provolone	American cheese food

1. To make sauce: In 4-quart Dutch oven over medium heat, cook **Meat**, onion, garlic and **Herb** until meat is browned and onion is tender, stirring to break up meat. Pour off fat. Stir in soup, water and tomato paste. Heat to boiling; reduce heat to low. Simmer, uncovered, 30 minutes or until desired consistency, stirring occasionally.

2. To make filling: In large bowl, combine ricotta cheese, **Cheese 1**, parsley and nutmeg; set aside.

3. Pat drained noodles dry with paper towels. On each noodle, spread about ⅓ cup of the cheese filling. Fold over 1 inch and roll up each noodle jelly-roll fashion.

4. Spread 2 cups of the meat sauce in 13- by 9-inch baking dish. Place rolls, seam side down, in dish. Spoon remaining sauce over rolls. Sprinkle with **Cheese 2**. Bake at 350°F. 45 minutes or until hot. Let stand 5 minutes before serving. Makes 8 servings.

Creamy Noodle Supper

2 tablespoons butter or margarine
⅓ cup chopped onion
1 can (10¾ ounces) condensed **Soup**
½ cup milk

⅛ teaspoon rubbed dried sage
⅛ teaspoon pepper
4 ounces (about 3 cups) medium
noodles, cooked and drained

Meat
1 cup drained, cooked **Vegetable**
Topping

Soup	Meat	Vegetable	Topping
cream of chicken	1½ cups diced cooked chicken	mixed vegetables	2 tablespoons buttered bread crumbs
cream of celery	1 can (about 7 ounces) tuna, drained and flaked	diced carrots	¼ cup toasted sliced almonds
cream of mushroom	1½ cups diced cooked beef	peas	½ cup shredded American cheese

1. Preheat oven to 400°F. In 3-quart saucepan over medium heat, in hot butter, cook onion until tender, stirring often. Stir in **Soup**, milk, sage and pepper until well mixed. Stir in noodles, **Meat** and **Vegetable** just until mixed. Turn into 1½-quart casserole.

2. Bake 20 minutes or until ... **Topping**. Ba...

To Microwave: In 1½-quart microwave-safe casserole, combine butter, onion and **Vegetable;** cover. Microwave on HIGH 3 to 5 minutes; until onion is tender, stirring once. Stir in **Soup**, milk, sage and pepper until well mixed. Stir in noodles and **Meat;** cover. Microwave on HIGH 6 to 8 minutes until hot, stirring once. Sprinkle with **Topping**. Microwave, uncovered, on HIGH 2 minutes more.

Lasagna Roll-Ups

Supper à la King

¼ cup butter or margarine
½ cup diced green pepper
⅓ cup chopped onion

1 can (10¾ ounces) condensed **Soup**
¾ cup milk
2 cups cubed cooked **Meat**

¾ cup shredded **Cheese**
¼ cup diced pimento
Accompaniment

Soup	Meat	Cheese	Accompaniment
cream of chicken	chicken	Swiss	shredded zucchini, cooked and drained
cream of asparagus	ham	Cheddar	baked potatoes, split
cream of mushroom	turkey	Muenster	cooked spaghetti squash (see **Tip** below)
cream of celery	kielbasa	American	biscuits, split

1. In 10-inch skillet over medium heat, in hot butter, cook green pepper and onion until tender, stirring occasionally. Stir in **Soup** and milk; blend well. Stir in **Meat**, **Cheese** and pimento. Cook 5 minutes more or until heated through.

2. Arrange **Accompaniment** on serving platter. Serve sauce over accompaniment. Makes about 3½ cups sauce, 6 servings.

To Microwave: Use ingredients as above but use only 2 tablespoons butter. In 2-quart microwave-safe casserole, combine only 2 tablespoons butter, green pepper and onion; cover. Microwave on HIGH 2 to 3 minutes until vegetables are tender. Stir in **Soup** and milk; blend well. Stir in **Meat**, **Cheese** and pimento; cover. Microwave on HIGH 7 to 9 minutes until hot, stirring occasionally. Serve as above.

Tip: To cook spaghetti squash: Halve squash lengthwise; remove seeds and stringy portions. In 10-inch skillet, place squash halves, cut side up. Add 1 inch water. Over medium heat, heat to boiling. Reduce heat to low. Cover; simmer 30 minutes or until fork-tender. Drain. With fork, scrape spaghetti-like strands from squash shell; place on serving platter. Discard shells.

Versatile Crepes

3 eggs
1 cup milk
⅔ cup all-purpose flour

Vegetable oil
1 can (10¾ to 11 ounces) condensed **Soup**

Liquid
1½ cups shredded **Cheese,** divided
Filling

Soup	Liquid	Cheese	Filling
cream of chicken	2 tablespoons dry sherry plus ⅓ cup water	sharp Cheddar	2 cups diced cooked chicken
cream of mushroom	½ cup milk	longhorn	1 can (15½ ounces) salmon, drained and flaked
Cheddar cheese	¼ cup dry white wine plus ¼ cup water	Swiss	2 cups diced cooked ham
cream of celery	½ cup light cream	Monterey Jack	2 cups drained, cooked chopped broccoli

1. In medium bowl, combine eggs, milk and flour; beat until smooth.

2. Over medium heat, heat 8-inch crepe pan or skillet. When hot, brush lightly with vegetable oil. Add scant ¼ cup of the batter to skillet, rotating pan to spread batter evenly. Cook until surface is dry and edges are browned. Turn over; cook other side a few seconds. Remove from pan, stacking crepes as they are made. Repeat to make 10 crepes, brushing pan with oil as needed.

3. Preheat oven to 350°F. In 2-quart saucepan over medium heat, heat **Soup** and **Liquid,** stirring to mix. Add 1 cup **Cheese**; stir until cheese melts. Stir 1 cup sauce into **Filling.** Spoon 3 tablespoons filling down center of each crepe. Roll up. Repeat with remaining crepes.

4. Arrange rolled crepes, seam side down, in 12- by 8-inch baking dish. Pour remaining sauce over all; sprinkle with remaining ½ cup **Cheese.** Cover. Bake 25 minutes or until heated through. Makes 5 servings.

Supper à la King

Quick Stovetop Supper

1 tablespoon butter or margarine
½ cup sliced mushrooms
¼ cup chopped onion

1 can (10¾ to 11 ounces) condensed
Soup
½ cup milk
½ teaspoon dry mustard

Meat
½ cup **Vegetable**
Accompaniment

Soup	Meat	Vegetable	Accompaniment
cream of mushroom	1 cup cooked ham cut into strips	drained, cooked peas	baked potatoes, split
cream of celery	4 ounces dried beef, rinsed and cut into strips	drained, cooked cut green beans	toast points
cream of chicken	1 cup cooked turkey cut into strips	drained, cooked diced carrots	hot cooked noodles
Cheddar cheese	1 can (about 7 ounces) tuna, drained and flaked	packed chopped fresh spinach leaves	baked patty shells

1. In 2-quart saucepan over medium heat, in hot butter, cook mushrooms and onion until tender, stirring occasionally.

2. Stir in **Soup,** milk and mustard until smooth. Stir in **Meat** and **Vegetable.** Heat through, stirring occasionally. Serve over **Accompaniment.** Makes about 2 cups, 4 servings.

To Microwave: In 2-quart microwave-safe casserole, combine butter, mushrooms and onion; cover. Microwave on HIGH 3 to 4 minutes until onion is tender, stirring once. Stir in **Soup,** milk and mustard until smooth. Stir in **Meat** and **Vegetable;** cover. Microwave on HIGH 5 to 6 minutes until heated through, stirring occasionally. Serve mixture over **Accompaniment.**

Main Dish Spoonbread

Meat
Vegetable
1 cup cornmeal
1¼ cups water

3 tablespoons butter or margarine
1 can (10¾ to 11 ounces) condensed
Soup
3 eggs, beaten

1 teaspoon baking powder
Seasoning
Syrup or butter

Meat	Vegetable	Soup	Seasoning
6 slices bacon, diced	¼ cup finely chopped onion	Cheddar cheese	dash ground red pepper
1 cup diced cooked ham plus 2 tablespoons butter or margarine	¼ cup chopped green pepper	cream of chicken	⅛ teaspoon paprika
½ pound bulk pork sausage	½ cup finely chopped celery	cream of celery	½ teaspoon rubbed dried sage
1 cup diced cooked corned beef plus 2 tablespoons vegetable oil	½ cup chopped mushrooms	cream of mushroom	⅛ teaspoon garlic powder

1. In 3-quart saucepan over medium heat, cook **Meat** until browned, stirring occasionally. Remove meat; drain on paper towels. In drippings, cook **Vegetable** until tender. Stir in cornmeal and water until smooth. Heat to boiling; stir constantly. Remove from heat.

2. Stir in butter until melted. Stir in **Soup,** eggs, baking powder, **Seasoning** and reserved meat. Pour into buttered 2-quart casserole. Bake at 350°F. 50 minutes or until knife inserted in center comes out clean. Serve with syrup or butter. Makes 6 servings.

Quick Stovetop Supper

Souper Enchiladas

½ cup vegetable oil
8 corn tortillas (6 inch)
1 cup chopped onion
1 large clove garlic, minced

1 can (11¼ to 11½ ounces)
condensed **Soup**
2 cups shredded cooked **Meat**
½ cup water

1 teaspoon ground cumin
Seasoning
1 jar (8 ounces) taco sauce
1 cup shredded **Cheese**

Soup	Meat	Seasoning	Cheese
bean with bacon	chicken	1 can (4 ounces) chopped green chilies, drained	Cheddar
chili beef	beef	¼ teaspoon hot pepper sauce	Monterey Jack

1. Preheat oven to 350°F. In 8-inch skillet over medium heat, in hot oil, fry tortillas, one at a time, 2 to 3 seconds on each side. Drain tortillas on paper towels.

2. Spoon about 2 tablespoons of the hot oil into 10-inch skillet. Over medium heat, in the 2 tablespoons oil, cook onion and garlic until tender, stirring occasionally. Stir in **Soup, Meat,** water, cumin and **Seasoning.** Heat through.

3. Spoon about ⅓ cup of the soup mixture onto each tortilla; roll up. Arrange filled tortillas in 12- by 8-inch baking dish. Pour taco sauce evenly over enchiladas. Sprinkle with **Cheese.** Cover. Bake 25 minutes. Uncover; bake 5 minutes more. Makes 4 servings.

To Microwave: Use ingredients as above but use only 1 tablespoon oil. In 2-quart microwave-safe casserole, combine only 1 tablespoon oil, onion and garlic; cover. Microwave on HIGH 2 to 3 minutes until tender. Stir in **Soup, Meat,** water, cumin and **Seasoning;** cover. Microwave on HIGH 4 to 6 minutes until heated through, stirring once. Let stand, covered. Meanwhile, wrap tortillas in paper towel and place in microwave oven. Microwave on HIGH 2 minutes or until tortillas are pliable. Assemble as in Step 3, placing filled tortillas in 12- by 8-inch microwave-safe dish. Pour taco sauce evenly over enchiladas; cover. Microwave on HIGH 8 to 10 minutes until hot, rotating dish once. Sprinkle with **Cheese.** Microwave on HIGH 2 to 3 minutes until cheese is melted.

Chimichangas

1 pound ground beef
1 medium onion, chopped
1 clove garlic, minced
1 can (10¾ to 11¼ ounces)
condensed **Soup**

1 can (4 ounces) chopped green
chilies, drained
1 tablespoon vinegar
1 teaspoon **Seasoning**
½ teaspoon ground cumin

8 flour tortillas (8 inch)
1 cup shredded **Cheese**
Vegetable oil
Shredded lettuce
Topping

Soup	Seasoning	Cheese	Topping
zesty tomato	dried oregano leaves, crushed	Monterey Jack	taco sauce
tomato rice	chili powder	American	chopped green onions
tomato	dried marjoram leaves, crushed	Provolone	chopped radishes
chili beef plus ½ cup water	dried basil leaves, crushed	longhorn	sour cream

1. In 10-inch skillet over medium heat, cook beef, onion and garlic until meat is browned; stir often to break up meat. Pour off fat. Stir in **Soup,** chilies, vinegar, **Seasoning** and cumin; reduce heat. Simmer 10 to 15 minutes or until most of the liquid evaporates. Cool slightly.

2. Spoon ¼ cup of the filling down center of one tortilla. Top with 2 tablespoons of the **Cheese.** Fold in sides of tortilla; roll up tortilla around filling. Secure with a toothpick. Assemble 2 or 3 at a time.

3. In 10-inch skillet, heat 1 inch oil to 350°F. Fry chimichangas 2 minutes or until golden, turning once. Remove and drain on paper towels. Garnish with lettuce and **Topping.** Makes 8 servings.

Tip: *To make burritos: Preheat oven to 350°F. Prepare filling as in Step 1. Spoon ¼ cup of the filling down center of one tortilla; top with 2 tablespoons of the* **Cheese.** *Roll tortilla around filling. Repeat with remaining tortillas and filling. Place on baking sheet; cover with foil. Bake 15 minutes or until hot. Garnish as above.*

Souper Enchiladas

Tostadas

1 can (11¼ ounces) condensed
chili beef soup
1 cup finely chopped cooked **Meat**
1 package (3 ounces) cream cheese,
cubed

½ teaspoon dried oregano leaves,
crushed
¼ cup water
Vegetable oil
6 corn tortillas (6 inch)
Shredded lettuce
Diced tomato

1 cup shredded **Cheese**
⅓ cup **Topping**
Taco sauce
Garnish

Meat	Cheese	Topping	Garnish
pork	Cheddar	guacamole	sliced pitted ripe olives
beef	Monterey Jack with jalapeño peppers	plain yogurt	chopped green onions
chicken	Monterey Jack	sour cream	chopped fresh cilantro or parsley
ham	Muenster	creamy blue cheese dressing	pickled peppers

1. In 2-quart saucepan over low heat, heat soup, **Meat,** cream cheese, oregano and water until hot, stirring occasionally.

2. In small skillet over medium heat, heat ½ inch oil to 350°F. Fry tortillas, one at a time, about 1 minute until golden brown, turning once. Remove and drain on paper towels.

3. Top each tostada shell with ¼ cup of the soup mixture. Top with lettuce, tomato, **Cheese, Topping** and taco sauce. Sprinkle with **Garnish.** Makes 6 servings.

To Microwave: Prepare tostada shells as in Step 2. While shells are draining, in 1½-quart microwave-safe casserole, combine soup, **Meat,** cream cheese, oregano and water; cover. Microwave on HIGH 5 to 8 minutes until hot, stirring occasionally. Proceed as in Step 3.

Tip: *Prepared tostada shells are available at your grocery store—heat according to package directions and top with filling and toppings.*

Tacos

Meat
½ cup chopped onion
2 cloves garlic, minced

1 tablespoon chili powder
1 can (10¾ to 11 ounces) condensed
Soup
8 taco shells

1 cup shredded **Cheese**
Shredded lettuce
1 cup **Addition**

Meat	Soup	Cheese	Addition
1 pound ground beef	tomato	Cheddar	chopped tomatoes
1 pound ground pork	tomato rice	Monterey Jack	chopped green onions
1 pound bulk pork sausage	zesty tomato	American	salsa

1. Preheat oven to 350°F. In 10-inch skillet over medium heat, cook **Meat,** onion, garlic and chili powder until meat is well browned, stirring to break up meat. Pour off fat. Stir in **Soup.** Heat through, stirring occasionally.

2. Place about ¼ cup of the meat mixture in each taco shell. Place on baking sheet. Bake 5 minutes. Top with **Cheese,** lettuce and **Addition.** Makes 8 tacos, 4 servings.

To Microwave: In 1½-quart microwave-safe casserole, crumble **Meat.** Add onion, garlic and chili powder; cover. Microwave on HIGH 6 to 8 minutes until meat is nearly done, stirring occasionally. Pour off fat. Stir in **Soup;** cover. Microwave on HIGH 2 to 3 minutes until heated through, stirring once. Place about ¼ cup of the meat mixture in each taco shell. In 12- by 8-inch microwave-safe dish, arrange taco shells. Microwave on HIGH 2 to 3 minutes. Top with **Cheese,** lettuce and **Addition.**

Tostadas

Stuffed Chicken Breasts

4 chicken breast halves
Meat
¼ cup chopped fresh parsley
2 tablespoons vegetable oil

¼ cup chopped onion
2 cloves garlic, minced
1 can (10¾ ounces) condensed **Soup**
½ cup **Wine**

¼ cup water
Dried **Herb**, crushed
Hot cooked rice

Meat	Soup	Wine	Herb
4 thin slices cooked ham	cream of chicken	dry sherry	⅛ teaspoon tarragon leaves
4 slices bacon, cooked	tomato	dry red wine	½ teaspoon basil leaves
4 slices dried beef, rinsed	cream of mushroom	dry vermouth	½ teaspoon marjoram leaves

1. Cut 3-inch slit in thick part of each breast half. Tuck 1 slice **Meat** and 1 tablespoon parsley into each slit; secure with toothpicks.

2. In 10-inch skillet over medium heat, in hot oil, cook chicken until browned on both sides. Remove chicken to platter. Pour off fat, reserving 1 tablespoon drippings in skillet.

3. Add onion and garlic to skillet; cook 2 minutes, stirring constantly. Stir in **Soup, Wine,** water and **Herb;** heat to boiling.

4. Return chicken to skillet. Reduce heat to low. Cover; simmer 30 minutes or until chicken is fork-tender.

5. Transfer chicken to platter; remove toothpicks. Skim fat from cooking liquid. Spoon some sauce over chicken; serve remaining sauce over rice. Makes 4 servings.

Lemon-Herbed Chicken

2 tablespoons vegetable oil
2 pounds chicken parts
1 can (10¾ ounces) condensed **Soup**

2 tablespoons lemon juice
½ teaspoon paprika
Seasoning

¼ teaspoon dried **Herb**
1 lemon, sliced
Accompaniment

Soup	Seasoning	Herb	Accompaniment
cream of chicken	⅛ teaspoon pepper	tarragon leaves, crushed	hot cooked rice
cream of celery	¼ teaspoon lemon-pepper seasoning	marjoram leaves, crushed	hot cooked noodles
cream of mushroom	¼ teaspoon dry mustard	rosemary leaves, crushed	hot mashed potatoes
creamy chicken mushroom	⅛ teaspoon ground red pepper	rubbed sage	hot stuffing

1. In 10-inch skillet over medium heat, in hot oil, cook chicken until browned on all sides. Pour off fat.

2. Stir in **Soup,** lemon juice, paprika, **Seasoning** and **Herb.** Heat to boiling; reduce heat to low. Cover; simmer 30 to 40 minutes or until chicken is tender, stirring occasionally. Garnish chicken with lemon slices. Serve with **Accompaniment.** Makes 4 servings.

To Microwave: Use ingredients as above but omit oil. In 12-by 8-inch microwave-safe dish, arrange chicken with thicker pieces toward edge of dish; cover. Microwave on HIGH 8 to 10 minutes, rotating dish once. Pour off fat and rearrange pieces. In small bowl, combine **Soup,** lemon juice, paprika, **Seasoning** and **Herb.** Spoon evenly over chicken; cover. Microwave on HIGH 8 to 10 minutes until chicken is fork-tender, rotating dish once. Let stand, covered, 2 to 5 minutes. Remove chicken to serving platter. Stir soup mixture until smooth and creamy. Pour over chicken. Top with lemon slices; serve with **Accompaniment.**

Stuffed Chicken Breasts

Oriental Skillet

1 pound **Cutlets**
¼ cup butter or margarine
½ cup green onions cut into ½-inch pieces
2 cloves garlic, minced

1 can (10¾ ounces) condensed chicken broth
Seasoning
Vegetable
½ cup sliced water chestnuts

1 to 2 tablespoons cornstarch
3 tablespoons water
Garnish

Cutlets	Seasoning	Vegetable	Garnish
turkey	¼ teaspoon ground ginger	1½ cups sliced broccoli	1 carrot, slivered
chicken	½ teaspoon lemon-pepper seasoning	1 cup fresh or frozen snow peas	2 tablespoons sliced pitted ripe olives
veal	¼ teaspoon Chinese five-spice powder	1 cup sliced zucchini	1 tablespoon chopped pimento

1. With mallet, pound **Cutlets** to ¼-inch thickness, if necessary. In 10-inch skillet over medium heat, in hot butter, cook until browned on both sides. Remove from skillet.

2. Add green onions and garlic to skillet; cook 2 minutes, stirring constantly. Add broth and **Seasoning;** heat to boiling. Add cutlets. Reduce heat to low. Cover; simmer 15 minutes or until nearly tender, stirring occasionally.

3. Stir in **Vegetable** and water chestnuts; simmer 5 minutes or until vegetable is tender.

4. Remove cutlets and vegetables to platter; keep warm. In cup, stir together cornstarch and water. Stir into juices in skillet. Over medium heat, heat to boiling, stirring constantly. Cook 1 minute more. Pour over cutlets and vegetables; top with **Garnish.** Makes 4 servings.

Sweet and Sour Skillet

1 can (8 ounces) pineapple chunks in juice
1 can (10½ to 10¾ ounces) condensed **Soup**
¼ cup packed brown sugar

1 tablespoon cornstarch
2 tablespoons vinegar
2 tablespoons soy sauce
2 tablespoons vegetable oil

Meat
Vegetable 1
½ cup **Vegetable 2**
Hot cooked rice

Soup	Meat	Vegetable 1	Vegetable 2
chicken with rice	12 ounces cooked ham, cut into strips	1 cup fresh or frozen snow peas	sweet red pepper strips
chicken gumbo	1 pound boneless raw chicken, cut into 1-inch pieces	2 cups thinly sliced broccoli flowerets	sliced bamboo shoots
French onion	1 pound medium shrimp, shelled and deveined	1 cup thinly sliced celery	sliced water chestnuts

1. Drain pineapple, reserving juice. In small bowl, combine pineapple juice, **Soup,** sugar, cornstarch, vinegar and soy sauce; set aside.

2. In 10-inch skillet over medium-high heat, in hot oil, stir-fry **Meat,** half at a time, until ham is lightly browned or meat is done. Remove with slotted spoon.

3. In same skillet, stir-fry **Vegetable 1** and **Vegetable 2** until tender-crisp. Stir soup mixture to blend; stir into skillet. Over medium heat, heat to boiling, stirring constantly.

4. Return meat to pan; cook 1 minute more or until hot. Serve over rice. Makes about 4 cups, 4 servings.

Oriental Skillet

Baked Chicken Florida

1 can (10½ to 10¾ ounces)
condensed **Soup**
Juice
¼ cup water

Seasoning
¼ teaspoon dried tarragon leaves,
crushed

3 pounds chicken parts
1 tablespoon cornstarch
Garnish

Soup	Juice	Seasoning	Garnish
chicken broth	¼ cup lemon juice	½ teaspoon minced fresh ginger	orange wedges
chicken with rice	¼ cup lime juice	1 clove garlic, minced	kiwi fruit slices

1. To make marinade: In small bowl, combine **Soup, Juice,** water, **Seasoning** and tarragon. In shallow baking dish, pour marinade over chicken. Cover; refrigerate at least 2 hours, turning chicken occasionally. Drain chicken, reserving marinade.

2. In shallow roasting pan, arrange chicken. Bake at 375°F. 50 minutes or until chicken is fork-tender, basting chicken frequently with marinade. Remove to serving platter; keep warm.

3. Pour remaining marinade and pan drippings into 1-quart saucepan; stir in cornstarch. Over medium heat, heat to boiling, stirring occasionally; cook 1 minute more. Spoon some sauce over chicken; pass remaining sauce. Arrange **Garnish** around chicken. Makes 6 servings.

Crispy Baked Chicken

1 can (10¾ to 11 ounces) condensed
Soup
Seasoning

½ cup water
Crumbs
¼ cup **Addition**

⅓ cup all-purpose flour
2 pounds chicken parts

Soup	Seasoning	Crumbs	Addition
Cheddar cheese	½ teaspoon dried oregano leaves, crushed	2 cups finely crushed corn flakes	sesame seed
cream of mushroom	¼ teaspoon rubbed dried sage	1½ cups seasoned fine dry bread crumbs	finely chopped walnuts
cream of chicken	½ teaspoon dried basil leaves, crushed	2 cups finely crushed potato chips	wheat germ
creamy chicken mushroom	1 teaspoon chili powder	2 cups finely crushed corn chips	finely chopped almonds

1. In deep pie plate, stir together **Soup, Seasoning** and water until smooth. On waxed paper, combine **Crumbs** and **Addition.** On second sheet of waxed paper, place flour. Coat chicken with flour, then soup mixture, then crumb mixture. Place on wire rack in jelly-roll pan.

2. Bake at 375°F. 50 minutes or until chicken is fork-tender. Makes 4 servings.

Tip: *Chicken may be skinned before coating, if desired.*

Cornish Hens and Vegetables

2 tablespoons vegetable oil
2 tablespoons butter or margarine
2 Cornish hens (about 1½ pounds each), split lengthwise

1 cup **Vegetable 1**
Vegetable 2
2 cloves garlic, minced
½ teaspoon dried **Herb,** crushed

1 can (10½ to 10¾ ounces) condensed **Soup**
1 tablespoon cornstarch
2 tablespoons cold water

Vegetable 1	Vegetable 2	Herb	Soup
sliced mushrooms	4 green onions, sliced	tarragon leaves	chicken broth
sliced zucchini	2 tablespoons chopped pimento	thyme leaves	French onion
chopped tomato	½ cup chopped onion	basil leaves	tomato

1. Preheat oven to 350°F. In 10-inch skillet over medium-high heat, in hot oil and butter, cook hens until browned on both sides, 2 halves at a time. Remove to 12- by 8-inch baking dish. Reserve drippings in skillet.

2. Reduce heat to medium. Add **Vegetable 1, Vegetable 2,** garlic and **Herb.** Cook 2 minutes, stirring constantly. Add **Soup;** heat to boiling. Pour hot mixture over hens. Cover.

3. Bake 25 minutes. Uncover; baste hens with pan juices. Bake, uncovered, 10 minutes more or until hens are fork-tender.

4. Remove hens to warm platter and keep warm. Pour pan juices into skillet; over high heat, heat to boiling. In cup, stir together cornstarch and water; stir into boiling liquid. Boil 1 minute. Spoon some sauce over hens; pass remaining sauce. Makes 4 servings.

Sautéed Chicken Livers

¼ cup butter or margarine
1 pound chicken livers
Flavoring

2 tablespoons all-purpose flour
1 can (10½ to 10¾ ounces) condensed **Soup**

½ cup water
Dash pepper
Accompaniment

Flavoring	Soup	Accompaniment
1 medium onion, coarsely chopped	chicken broth	hot cooked noodles
1 cup sliced mushrooms	French onion	baked potatoes, split
1 large green pepper, cut into strips	chicken gumbo	hot cooked rice

1. In 10-inch skillet over medium-high heat, in hot butter, cook livers and **Flavoring** 8 to 10 minutes until livers are done, stirring frequently.

2. With slotted spoon, remove livers and flavoring from skillet. Into pan drippings, stir flour. Gradually add **Soup,** water and pepper, stirring constantly. Over medium heat, heat to boiling, stirring occasionally. Cook 1 minute more.

3. Add liver mixture; heat through. Serve over **Accompaniment.** Makes about 3 cups, 4 servings.

Pasta with Shrimp Sauce

¼ cup vegetable oil
2 cups sliced mushrooms
¾ cup chopped onion
2 cloves garlic, minced

½ pound medium shrimp, shelled
and deveined
Seafood
1 can (10¾ to 11 ounces) condensed
Soup

Liquid
¼ cup chopped fresh parsley
8 ounces **Pasta**, cooked and drained
Grated Parmesan cheese

Seafood	Soup	Liquid	Pasta
½ pound bay scallops	Cheddar cheese	1 cup half-and-half	linguine
1 can (6½ ounces) minced clams, drained	cream of celery	¼ cup dry sherry plus ¼ cup milk	spaghetti
½ pound cod or other fish, cut into chunks	tomato	¼ cup dry white wine plus ¼ cup milk	medium noodles
½ pound additional shrimp	cream of mushroom	1 cup tomato juice	small shell macaroni

1. In 10-inch skillet over medium heat, in hot oil, cook mushrooms, onion and garlic until tender, stirring occasionally. Add shrimp and **Seafood**; cook 2 minutes more until seafood is done, stirring constantly.

2. In medium bowl, combine **Soup** and **Liquid**; mix well. Stir into skillet; add parsley. Heat through but do not boil. Serve sauce over hot cooked **Pasta**. Pass grated Parmesan cheese. Makes 4 servings.

Wine-Sauced Seafood

¼ cup butter or margarine
1 cup soft bread crumbs
1 cup sliced mushrooms
Vegetable

Seasoning
Seafood
2 cups **Rice/Pasta**
1 can (10¾ ounces) condensed cream
of mushroom soup

½ cup milk
¼ cup dry white wine
1 tablespoon chopped pimento
(optional)

Vegetable	Seasoning	Seafood	Rice/Pasta
1 green pepper, chopped	½ teaspoon paprika	1 pound firm fish fillets, cut into 1-inch pieces	cooked rice
1 cup sliced celery	½ teaspoon dried thyme leaves, crushed	1 pound bay scallops	cooked small shell macaroni
1 cup cut asparagus	½ teaspoon dried dill weed, crushed	½ pound cooked crab meat	cooked fine egg noodles
4 cups chopped fresh spinach leaves	⅛ teaspoon ground nutmeg	1 can (15½ ounces) salmon, drained and broken into chunks	cooked wild rice

1. Preheat oven to 400°F. In 10-inch skillet over medium heat, melt butter. In small bowl, toss 1 tablespoon of the melted butter with bread crumbs; set aside.

2. In remaining butter, cook mushrooms, **Vegetable** and **Seasoning** until tender; stir often. Add **Seafood**; cook 2 minutes more, stirring often. Remove from heat.

3. Divide **Rice/Pasta** into four 12-ounce casseroles. Divide seafood mixture into casseroles. In same skillet, stir together soup, milk and wine until smooth. Over medium heat, heat to boiling, stirring constantly. Stir in pimento; pour over seafood mixture. Sprinkle with buttered bread crumbs. Bake 20 minutes or until lightly browned. Makes 4 servings.

Pasta with Shrimp Sauce

Salmon and Noodle Skillet

1 can (15½ ounces) salmon, drained and flaked
1 can (10¾ to 11 ounces) condensed **Soup**, divided
Crumbs

2 tablespoons finely chopped onion
2 tablespoons chopped fresh parsley
1 tablespoon lemon juice
1 egg, beaten
Vegetable
2 tablespoons butter or margarine

½ cup sour cream
½ cup milk
4 ounces (about 3 cups) medium noodles, cooked and drained
Seasoning

Soup	Crumbs	Vegetable	Seasoning
cream of celery	1 cup soft bread crumbs	2 cups fresh or frozen cut asparagus	½ teaspoon dried dill weed, crushed
cream of mushroom	½ cup finely crushed saltine crackers	2 cups fresh or frozen cut green beans	½ teaspoon dried marjoram leaves, crushed
cream of chicken	½ cup fine dry bread crumbs	2 cups fresh or frozen cut broccoli	¼ teaspoon ground nutmeg
Cheddar cheese	¼ cup quick-cooking oats	1 cup fresh or frozen peas	2 tablespoons grated Parmesan cheese

1. In medium bowl, combine salmon, ¼ cup of the **Soup, Crumbs,** onion, parsley, lemon juice and egg; mix well. Shape into 4 patties, each about 1 inch thick.

2. In 10-inch skillet over medium heat, in ½ inch boiling water, cook **Vegetable** until tender-crisp; drain in colander.

3. In same skillet over medium heat, in hot butter, cook salmon patties until browned on both sides. Remove from skillet.

4. In same skillet, combine remaining **Soup,** sour cream and milk, stirring until smooth. Stir in noodles, **Seasoning** and cooked vegetable. Arrange salmon patties over noodle mixture. Cover; cook over low heat 10 minutes or until heated through. Do not boil. Makes 4 servings.

Perfect Tuna Casserole

1 can (10¾ ounces) condensed **Soup**
¼ cup milk

1 can (about 7 ounces) tuna, drained and flaked
2 hard-cooked eggs, sliced

1 cup drained, cooked **Vegetable**
Topper

Soup	Vegetable	Topper
cream of mushroom	peas	3 slices American cheese, cut into slivers
cream of celery	cut green beans	¼ cup toasted sliced almonds
New England clam chowder	cut broccoli	1 medium tomato, sliced

1. Preheat oven to 350°F. In 1-quart casserole, stir together **Soup** and milk until well mixed. Stir in tuna, eggs and **Vegetable.**

2. Bake 25 minutes or until hot; stir. Garnish with **Topper;** bake 5 minutes more. Makes 4 servings.

To Microwave: In 1-quart microwave-safe casserole, stir together **Soup** and milk. Stir in tuna, eggs and **Vegetable;** cover. Microwave on HIGH 8 to 10 minutes until hot, stirring occasionally. Garnish with **Topper.** Microwave on HIGH 1 to 3 minutes more until heated through.

Tip: *Toast almonds while the casserole is cooking in Step 2. Simply spread almonds in a shallow baking pan and bake alongside the casserole 5 to 10 minutes until almonds are golden, stirring once or twice.*

Vegetable-Stuffed Fish Rolls

½ cup chopped tomato
½ cup chopped mushrooms
¼ cup chopped green onions

1 can (10¾ to 11 ounces) condensed
Soup, divided
6 **Fish** fillets (1½ pounds)

¼ cup **Liquid**
1 cup shredded **Cheese**

Soup	Fish	Liquid	Cheese
cream of mushroom	sole	dry white wine	Swiss
Cheddar cheese	flounder	milk	sharp Cheddar
cream of celery	haddock	water	Muenster

1. Preheat oven to 350°F. In medium bowl, combine tomato, mushrooms, green onions and ¼ cup of the **Soup**. Place about 3 tablespoons of the mixture on each **Fish** fillet and roll up. Secure with toothpicks if needed. Place fish rolls, seam side down, in 10- by 6-inch baking dish. Bake 25 minutes or until fish flakes easily when tested with fork. Discard any liquid in baking dish.

2. Meanwhile, in 2-quart saucepan, combine remaining **Soup** and **Liquid**. Over medium heat, heat through. Pour sauce over fish rolls; sprinkle with **Cheese**.

3. Bake 2 minutes more or until cheese is melted. Makes 6 servings.

To Microwave: In medium bowl, combine tomato, mushrooms, green onions and ¼ cup of the **Soup**. Fill and roll **Fish** as directed. Place fish rolls, seam side down, in 10- by 6-inch microwave-safe dish; cover. Microwave on HIGH 8 to 14 minutes until fish flakes easily when tested with fork, rotating dish twice. Discard any liquid in dish. Let stand, covered, 2 to 3 minutes. Meanwhile, in 2-cup glass measure, combine remaining **Soup** and **Liquid**. Microwave on HIGH 2 minutes or until hot. Pour sauce over fish rolls; top with **Cheese**. Microwave on HIGH 1 minute more or until cheese is melted.

Brown Rice Supper

2 tablespoons vegetable oil
Meat
½ cup **Vegetable**
1 medium onion, sliced

1 clove garlic, minced
1 cup brown rice, uncooked
1 can (10½ to 10¾ ounces)
condensed **Soup**

1 can (14½ ounces) stewed tomatoes
½ cup water
1 teaspoon dried **Herb**, crushed

Meat	Vegetable	Soup	Herb
2 pounds chicken thighs and drumsticks	chopped green pepper	chicken broth	basil leaves
4 pork chops, each cut ½ inch thick	sliced mushrooms	beef broth	thyme leaves
4 smoked pork chops, each cut ½ inch thick	chopped celery	chicken gumbo	marjoram leaves
1 pound shrimp, peeled and deveined	sliced zucchini	chicken with rice	tarragon leaves

1. In 6-quart Dutch oven over medium heat, in hot oil, cook chicken or pork until browned on all sides. (Do not cook shrimp.) Remove from pan.

2. To drippings, add **Vegetable**, onion and garlic; cook until vegetables are tender, stirring frequently. Add rice; cook 1 minute, stirring constantly. Stir in **Soup**, tomatoes with their liquid, water and **Herb**.

3. Arrange chicken or pork over rice (do not add shrimp). Heat to boiling. Reduce heat to low. Cover; simmer 1 hour or until rice is tender, stirring occasionally. Add more water during cooking, if mixture appears dry. (If using shrimp, add during last 10 minutes cooking time.) Uncover; let stand 5 minutes before serving. Makes 4 servings.

Tip: *Use white rice instead of brown rice to make this dish more quickly. Prepare as above, but substitute 1 cup uncooked regular rice for brown rice. In Step 3, simmer 30 to 40 minutes until meat is tender.*

Cheese Plus Sandwiches

1 package (3 ounces) cream cheese, softened
1 can (11 ounces) condensed Cheddar cheese soup/sauce

Seasoning
Bread
Lettuce leaves

Sliced tomato
Protein
Garnish

Seasoning	Bread	Protein	Garnish
1 tablespoon prepared horseradish	8 slices pumpernickel	2 cans (3¾ ounces each) sardines, drained	red onion rings
1 tablespoon prepared mustard	8 slices rye	8 slices cooked ham	dill pickle slices
1 tablespoon finely chopped jalapeño peppers	4 pita rounds, halved	1 can (about 15 ounces) red kidney beans, drained	diced avocado
¼ teaspoon ground ginger	8 slices whole wheat	8 slices cooked turkey	sliced peaches

1. In small bowl with mixer at medium speed, beat cream cheese until smooth. Beat in soup and **Seasoning** until well mixed.

2. Spread cheese mixture evenly onto one side of each **Bread** slice (or spread inside of pita bread). Top with lettuce, tomato, **Protein** and **Garnish.** Makes 8 servings.

Scrambled Eggs in Pita Pockets

4 pita bread rounds, halved
8 eggs
1 can (10¾ ounces) condensed **Soup**

1 cup **Vegetable**
Meat

2 tablespoons butter or margarine
1 cup shredded **Cheese**

Soup	Vegetable	Meat	Cheese
cream of mushroom	sliced mushrooms	6 slices bacon, diced	Cheddar
cream of celery	diced tomatoes	1 cup diced cooked ham plus 2 tablespoons vegetable oil	American
cream of chicken	chopped green pepper	¼ pound bulk pork sausage	Monterey Jack

1. Wrap pita bread in aluminum foil; bake at 350°F. 15 minutes or until warm.

2. Meanwhile, in bowl with whisk or rotary beater, beat eggs until foamy. Stir in **Soup** and **Vegetable;** set aside.

3. In 10-inch skillet over medium heat, cook bacon or pork sausage until done, or cook ham until heated through, stirring occasionally. Pour off fat.

4. Add butter to skillet; heat until foamy. Add egg mixture; cook until set but still slightly moist, stirring and lifting eggs so uncooked portion flows to bottom.

5. Stuff warm pita pockets with egg mixture. Add **Cheese** to each. Makes 8 servings.

Tip: *Buy pita bread rounds in the bakery or delicatessen section of your supermarket. They are usually available in white and whole wheat varieties. Cut them in half crosswise for stuffing.*

Cheese Plus Sandwiches

Cheese Omelet Roll

Vegetable oil
All-purpose flour
1 can (10¾ to 11 ounces) condensed **Soup**

6 eggs, separated
¼ teaspoon cream of tartar

1 cup shredded **Cheese**
Meat
1 cup **Vegetable**

Soup	Cheese	Meat	Vegetable
cream of celery	Cheddar	½ pound bacon, cooked, drained and crumbled	drained, cooked chopped broccoli
cream of chicken	Monterey Jack	½ pound bulk pork sausage, cooked, drained and crumbled	finely chopped fresh spinach leaves
Cheddar cheese	Swiss	1 cup diced cooked ham	drained, cooked chopped asparagus

1. Preheat oven to 350°F. Oil 15- by 10-inch jelly-roll pan; line with aluminum foil, extending 3 inches beyond pan on each end. Oil and flour bottom and sides of foil.

2. In 1-quart saucepan over medium heat, heat **Soup**, stirring occasionally. Remove from heat. In small bowl with fork, beat egg yolks. Stir some of hot soup into yolks, then return to soup. Over low heat, cook 1 minute, stirring constantly. Remove from heat.

3. In large bowl with mixer at high speed, beat egg whites and cream of tartar until stiff peaks form. Fold soup mixture into whites. Spread in prepared pan. Bake 20 to 25 minutes until puffy and browned.

4. Invert onto waxed paper; gently remove foil (some omelet may stick to foil). Sprinkle with **Cheese, Meat** and **Vegetable.** With aid of waxed paper, roll up jelly-roll fashion, starting at narrow side. Roll onto serving plate. Serve at once. Makes 6 servings.

Tip: *This omelet is delicious served plain, with stewed tomatoes or with a cheese sauce.*

Eggs Goldenrod

1 can (10¾ ounces) condensed **Soup**
½ cup **Liquid**

2 tablespoons chopped fresh parsley
¼ teaspoon dry mustard

4 hard-cooked eggs
Bread

Soup	Liquid	Bread
cream of celery	milk	4 slices toast
cream of chicken	chicken broth	4 English muffins, split and toasted
cream of mushroom	water	4 biscuits, split

1. In small saucepan, stir together **Soup, Liquid,** parsley and mustard until smooth.

2. Separate egg yolks and whites. Chop whites coarsely; add to soup mixture. Over medium heat, heat through, stirring occasionally.

3. Meanwhile, force egg yolks through sieve. Serve soup mixture on **Bread**, using about ½ cup per serving; garnish with sieved yolks. Makes about 2 cups, 4 servings.

To Microwave: In 1½-quart microwave-safe casserole, stir together **Soup, Liquid,** parsley and mustard; cover. Microwave on HIGH 2 to 3 minutes until hot, stirring once. Meanwhile, separate eggs and chop whites as in Step 2. Add whites to soup mixture; cover. Microwave on HIGH 1 to 2 minutes until heated through; stir. Serve as in Step 3.

Tip: *Make this dish a little more special by sprinkling it with fresh alfalfa sprouts.*

Cheese Omelet Roll

Souper Easy Quiche

| 4 eggs
1 can (10¾ to 11 ounces) condensed **Soup** | ½ cup light cream
1 cup shredded **Cheese**
Meat | ½ cup **Vegetable**
1 9-inch unbaked piecrust
Ground nutmeg |

Soup	Cheese	Meat	Vegetable
Cheddar cheese	sharp Cheddar	½ cup diced cooked ham	drained, cooked chopped broccoli
cream of mushroom	American	6 slices bacon, cooked, drained and crumbled	drained, cooked cut asparagus
cream of chicken	Monterey Jack	½ cup diced cooked chicken	sliced mushrooms
cream of celery	Swiss	½ cup diced cooked turkey	drained, cooked chopped spinach

1. In medium bowl, beat eggs until foamy. Gradually add **Soup** and cream, mixing well.

2. Sprinkle **Cheese, Meat** and **Vegetable** evenly over piecrust. Pour soup mixture over all. Sprinkle with nutmeg.

3. Bake at 350°F. 50 minutes or until center is set. Let stand 10 minutes before serving. Makes 6 servings.

Tip: *To make piecrust: In medium bowl, stir together 1 cup all-purpose flour and ½ teaspoon salt. With pastry blender, cut in ⅓ cup shortening until mixture resembles coarse crumbs. Add 2 to 3 tablespoons cold water, a tablespoon at a time, mixing lightly with fork until pastry holds together. Form into a ball. On lightly floured surface, roll dough to a 13-inch round. Transfer to 9-inch pie plate. Trim edge, leaving ½ inch pastry beyond edge of pie plate. Fold overhang under pastry; pinch to form a high edge. Flute edge.*

Easy Soufflé

| 1 can (10½ to 11 ounces) condensed **Soup** | 1 cup shredded **Cheese** | **Seasoning**
6 eggs, separated |

Soup	Cheese	Seasoning
Cheddar cheese	sharp Cheddar	dash ground red pepper
cream of asparagus	Swiss	⅛ teaspoon ground nutmeg
tomato	American	¼ teaspoon dried marjoram leaves, crushed
cream of chicken	Jarlsberg	2 tablespoons chopped fresh parsley

1. In 1-quart saucepan, combine **Soup, Cheese** and **Seasoning.** Over low heat, heat until cheese melts, stirring occasionally. Do not boil. Remove from heat.

2. In large bowl with mixer at high speed, beat egg whites until stiff peaks form; set aside. In small bowl with mixer at high speed, beat egg yolks until thick and lemon-colored. Gradually stir in soup mixture; fold into egg whites.

3. Pour into ungreased 2-quart casserole or soufflé dish. Bake at 300°F. 1 hour or until soufflé is lightly browned. Serve immediately. Makes 6 servings.

Souper Easy Quiche

Accompaniments

Company Cauliflower

1 large head (about 1½ pounds) cauliflower, cut into flowerets
2 tablespoons butter or margarine
½ cup chopped green pepper

1 cup sliced mushrooms
1 can (10¾ to 11 ounces) condensed **Soup**

Liquid
Cheese
1 tablespoon chopped pimento
Topping

Soup	Liquid	Cheese	Topping
Cheddar cheese	½ cup chicken broth	1 cup shredded Cheddar	chopped fresh parsley
cream of celery	½ cup milk	1 cup shredded Swiss	toasted sesame seed
cream of mushroom	⅓ cup light cream plus 2 tablespoons dry white wine	½ cup grated Romano	buttered bread crumbs
cream of chicken	½ cup water	¼ cup crumbled blue cheese	sliced almonds

1. In covered 10-inch skillet over medium heat, in 1 inch boiling water, cook cauliflower 10 minutes or until tender-crisp. Remove from heat; drain in colander.

2. In same skillet over medium heat, in hot butter, cook green pepper and mushrooms until tender, stirring occasionally. Stir in **Soup** and **Liquid;** mix well. Stir in **Cheese** and pimento.

3. Return cauliflower to skillet; heat through. Sprinkle with **Topping** before serving. Makes about 5 cups, 8 servings.

To Microwave: Use ingredients as above but omit **Liquid.** In 2-quart microwave-safe casserole, combine cauliflower and ¼ cup water; cover. Microwave on HIGH 6 to 8 minutes until tender-crisp, stirring twice. Let stand, covered, 2 to 3 minutes. Drain in colander. In same casserole, combine butter, green pepper and mushrooms; cover. Microwave on HIGH 3 to 5 minutes until green pepper is tender, stirring once. Stir in **Soup, Cheese,** pimento and cauliflower; cover. Microwave on HIGH 5 to 8 minutes until heated through, stirring occasionally. Sprinkle with **Topping.**

Curried Vegetables

1 can (10¾ ounces) condensed **Soup**
⅓ cup milk

½ teaspoon curry powder

4 cups drained, cooked **Vegetable**
Garnish

Soup	Vegetable	Garnish
cream of chicken	cut broccoli	½ cup French-fried onions
cream of celery	cut green beans	2 tablespoons toasted slivered almonds
cream of mushroom	cauliflowerets	2 tablespoons chopped peanuts

1. In 3-quart saucepan, stir together **Soup,** milk and curry powder until smooth.

2. Stir in **Vegetable.** Over medium heat, heat through, stirring occasionally. Pour into serving dish; sprinkle with **Garnish.** Makes about 4 cups, 6 servings.

To Microwave: In 2-quart microwave-safe casserole, stir together **Soup,** milk and curry powder until smooth. Stir in **Vegetable;** cover. Microwave on HIGH 4 to 6 minutes until heated through, stirring occasionally. Sprinkle with **Garnish.**

Company Cauliflower

Broccoli and Noodles Parmesan

1 bunch (about 1½ pounds) broccoli
2 tablespoons butter or margarine
½ cup chopped onion
1 clove garlic, minced

1 can (10¾ to 11 ounces) condensed
Soup
Seasoning
1 cup shredded **Cheese**

½ cup grated Parmesan cheese
1 cup **Dairy**
8 ounces (about 6 cups) noodles,
cooked and drained

Soup	Seasoning	Cheese	Dairy
cream of mushroom	½ teaspoon dried tarragon leaves, crushed	American	sour cream
cream of celery	½ teaspoon dried basil leaves, crushed	Cheddar	plain yogurt
cream of chicken	½ teaspoon curry powder	Swiss	ricotta cheese
Cheddar cheese	¼ teaspoon ground red pepper	Monterey Jack	creamed small curd cottage cheese

1. Cut broccoli into bite-sized pieces. In covered 4-quart saucepan over medium heat, in 1 inch boiling water, cook broccoli 6 minutes or until tender. Drain in colander.

2. In same saucepan over medium heat, in hot butter, cook onion and garlic until tender, stirring occasionally. Stir in **Soup** and **Seasoning;** mix well.

3. Add **Cheese** and Parmesan, stirring until melted. Stir in **Dairy,** broccoli and cooked noodles. Pour into 2-quart casserole. Cover; bake at 350°F. 30 minutes or until bubbly. Makes 8 servings.

To Microwave: Cut broccoli into bite-sized pieces. In 3-quart microwave-safe casserole, combine broccoli and ½ cup water; cover. Microwave on HIGH 6 to 8 minutes until almost tender. Let stand, covered, 2 to 3 minutes. Drain in colander. In same casserole, combine butter, onion and garlic; cover. Microwave on HIGH 2 to 2½ minutes until onion is tender. Stir in **Soup, Seasoning, Cheese** and Parmesan. Stir in **Dairy,** broccoli and cooked noodles; cover. Microwave on HIGH 8 to 10 minutes until heated through, stirring occasionally. Let stand, covered, 2 to 3 minutes.

Scalloped Vegetables

1 can (10¾ to 11 ounces) condensed
Soup
½ cup milk

¼ cup chopped fresh parsley
Dash pepper
4 cups **Vegetable 1**

Vegetable 2
1 tablespoon butter or margarine
Garnish

Soup	Vegetable 1	Vegetable 2	Garnish
cream of mushroom	thinly sliced potatoes	1 small onion, thinly sliced	paprika
cream of celery	sliced cauliflower	½ cup thinly sliced celery	pimento strips
cream of chicken	fresh or frozen whole kernel corn	½ cup finely chopped green pepper	crumbled cooked bacon
Cheddar cheese	thinly sliced turnips	½ cup thinly sliced carrots	shredded Cheddar cheese

1. In small bowl, combine **Soup,** milk, parsley and pepper. In 1½-quart casserole, arrange alternate layers of **Vegetable 1, Vegetable 2** and soup mixture, ending with soup mixture. Dot with butter; cover.

2. Bake at 375°F. 1 hour. Uncover; bake 15 minutes more or until vegetables are tender. Sprinkle with **Garnish.** Makes 6 servings.

To Microwave: Prepare as above in Step 1 but assemble in 2-quart microwave-safe casserole; cover. Microwave on HIGH 18 to 22 minutes until vegetables are tender, rotating dish 2 or 3 times. Sprinkle with **Garnish.**

Broccoli and Noodles Parmesan

Skillet Potatoes

3 tablespoons butter or margarine
1 cup **Vegetable 1**
½ cup **Vegetable 2**
2 cloves garlic, minced

1 can (10¾ ounces) condensed
chicken broth
¼ cup water
4 cups cubed potatoes

1 cup carrots cut into julienne strips
Seasoning
Garnish

Vegetable 1	Vegetable 2	Seasoning	Garnish
sliced celery	chopped onion	⅛ teaspoon pepper	chopped fresh parsley
frozen French-style green beans, thawed	sliced green onions with tops	¼ teaspoon dried thyme leaves, crushed	chopped fresh chives
sliced mushrooms	chopped leeks	⅛ teaspoon dry mustard	toasted sesame seed
chopped tomatoes	chopped green pepper	⅛ teaspoon crushed red pepper	chopped pimento

1. In 10-inch skillet over medium heat, in hot butter, cook **Vegetable 1, Vegetable 2** and garlic until vegetables are tender, stirring occasionally.

2. Add broth, water, potatoes, carrots and **Seasoning** to skillet. Heat to boiling; reduce heat to low. Cover; simmer 15 minutes or until potatoes are tender.

3. Uncover; over medium heat, simmer 5 minutes or until broth is slightly thickened, stirring often. Sprinkle with **Garnish** before serving. Makes about 5 cups, 6 servings.

Potato Boats

6 large baking potatoes
Vegetable oil
2 tablespoons butter or margarine

Seasoning
1 can (11 ounces) condensed Cheddar
cheese soup/sauce

2 tablespoons **Addition**
Garnish

Seasoning	Addition	Garnish
4 slices bacon, cooked, drained and crumbled	chopped green onions	paprika
½ teaspoon dried thyme leaves, crushed	chopped fresh parsley	ground nutmeg
⅛ teaspoon ground red pepper	chopped fresh chives	toasted sesame seed
2 teaspoons prepared mustard	chopped pimento	shredded Cheddar cheese

1. Scrub potatoes; rub lightly with oil. With fork, prick potatoes; place on baking sheet. Bake at 400°F. about 1 hour until potatoes are fork-tender.

2. With knife, cut off tops of potatoes. Scoop out pulp from each, leaving a thin shell. In medium bowl with mixer at medium speed, mash potato pulp with butter and **Seasoning**. Gradually add soup and **Addition**; beat until light and fluffy. Spoon potato mixture into shells. Sprinkle with **Garnish.**

3. Place potatoes on baking sheet. Bake at 450°F. 15 minutes or until hot. Makes 6 servings.

To Microwave: Use ingredients as above, but omit vegetable oil. Scrub potatoes; prick with fork. In 12- by 8-inch microwave-safe dish, arrange potatoes. Microwave on HIGH 20 to 25 minutes until potatoes are almost done, turning over and rearranging potatoes once. Let stand, covered, 5 to 10 minutes. Proceed as in Step 2. Place stuffed shells in same dish. Microwave on HIGH 7 to 10 minutes until hot, rearranging potatoes once.

Tip: *These potatoes can be baked and stuffed in advance. Omit the final baking time; cover and refrigerate until needed. Bake stuffed potatoes at 400°F. 30 minutes or until hot.*

Skillet Potatoes

Stuffed Vegetables

Vegetable
3 slices bacon, diced
1½ cups chopped mushrooms
½ cup chopped green onions

1 can (10¾ to 11 ounces) condensed
Soup, divided
1 cup fresh or frozen whole kernel
corn

Cheese
¼ cup milk
¼ teaspoon dried **Herb**, crushed
Paprika

Vegetable	Soup	Cheese	Herb
3 zucchini, halved lengthwise	cream of mushroom	½ cup shredded Swiss	tarragon leaves
3 green peppers, halved lengthwise	cream of celery	¼ cup grated Parmesan	summer savory leaves
6 medium tomatoes with ½-inch slice removed from top	Cheddar cheese	½ cup shredded sharp Cheddar	basil leaves

1. Preheat oven to 350°F. Remove seeds and pulp, if any, from **Vegetable,** leaving ¼-inch shell. In 10-inch skillet over medium heat, in 1 inch boiling water, cook zucchini shells or peppers 2 minutes. (Do not cook tomatoes; invert tomato shells on paper towels to drain.) Drain well. Discard water.

2. In same skillet over medium heat, cook bacon until crisp. Remove with slotted spoon; drain on paper towels. In bacon drippings, cook mushrooms and green onions un-til tender, stirring occasionally. Remove from heat. Stir in ½ cup of the **Soup**, corn, **Cheese** and reserved bacon.

3. In 12- by 8-inch baking dish, arrange vegetable shells. Spoon corn mixture into shells. Bake 20 minutes or until heated through.

4. Meanwhile, in small saucepan, combine remaining **Soup**, milk and **Herb**. Over low heat, heat just until hot, stirring occasionally. Spoon sauce over stuffed vegetables; sprinkle with paprika. Makes 6 servings.

Honey-Glazed Vegetables

1 can (10½ to 10¾ ounces)
condensed **Soup**
¼ cup honey

1 tablespoon cornstarch
1 teaspoon grated orange peel
⅛ teaspoon ground **Spice**

Vegetable
Garnish

Soup	Spice	Vegetable	Garnish
beef broth	cinnamon	2 pounds sweet potatoes, cooked, drained, peeled and cut into lengthwise quarters	slivered orange peel
French onion	nutmeg	2 pounds carrots, sliced, cooked and drained	grated Parmesan cheese
chicken broth	ginger	2 large acorn squash, cooked, drained and cut into ½-inch slices	raisins
chicken gumbo	cardamom	2 pounds parsnips, peeled, sliced, cooked and drained	chopped peanuts

1. In 10-inch skillet, combine **Soup**, honey, cornstarch, grated orange peel and **Spice**. Over medium heat, cook until thickened, stirring constantly.

2. Add **Vegetable**. Over low heat, cook 10 minutes or until vegetable is glazed, basting frequently. Turn into serving bowl; top with **Garnish**. Makes 6 servings.

To Microwave: Cook **Vegetable** according to microwave manufacturer's directions. In 3-quart microwave-safe casserole, combine **Soup**, honey, cornstarch, grated orange peel and **Spice**. Microwave on HIGH 4 minutes or until boiling and thickened, stirring twice. Add vegetable; cover. Microwave on HIGH 4 to 8 minutes until vegetable is glazed, stirring occasionally. Top with **Garnish**.

Macaroni and Cheese

1 can (10¾ to 11 ounces) condensed **Soup**
¾ cup **Liquid**

1 teaspoon prepared mustard
⅛ teaspoon pepper
6 ounces (about 1½ cups) elbow macaroni, cooked and drained

2 cups shredded **Cheese**, divided
Topper

Soup	Liquid	Cheese	Topper
cream of mushroom	milk	Cheddar	1 cup French-fried onions
cream of chicken	water	American	½ cup coarsely crushed potato chips
cream of celery	evaporated milk	Swiss	¼ cup buttered bread crumbs
Cheddar cheese	tomato juice	Monterey Jack	1 medium tomato, sliced

1. Preheat oven to 400°F. In 1½-quart casserole, stir together **Soup, Liquid,** mustard and pepper. Stir in macaroni and 1½ cups of the **Cheese.** Bake 20 minutes or until hot; stir.

2. Sprinkle with remaining ½ cup **Cheese** and **Topper;** bake 5 minutes more or until cheese melts. Makes 6 servings.

To Microwave: In 2-quart microwave-safe casserole, stir together **Soup, Liquid,** mustard, pepper, macaroni and 1½ cups of the **Cheese;** cover. Microwave on HIGH 7 to 10 minutes until hot, stirring occasionally. Sprinkle with remaining ½ cup **Cheese** and **Topper.** Microwave, uncovered, on HIGH 30 to 45 seconds until cheese melts.

Tip: *To make buttered crumbs: Toss ¼ cup fine dry bread crumbs with 1 tablespoon butter or margarine, melted. You can buy dry crumbs in your supermarket or make them at home. For homemade crumbs, bake bread slices at 300°F. about 20 minutes until very dry. Cool; crush with a rolling pin or in a blender.*

Cheesy Noodles

8 ounces (about 6 cups) wide noodles
¼ cup butter or margarine

1 can (10¾ to 11 ounces) condensed **Soup**
Liquid

Cheese
Garnish

Soup	Liquid	Cheese	Garnish
cream of mushroom	¾ cup milk	½ cup grated Parmesan	grated Parmesan cheese
cream of celery	¾ cup evaporated milk	½ cup grated Romano	poppy seed
Cheddar cheese	¾ cup light cream	½ cup shredded Gruyère	chopped fresh parsley
creamy chicken mushroom	¾ cup sour cream plus ¼ cup milk	1 cup shredded Cheddar	sliced pitted ripe olives

1. In 4-quart saucepan over high heat, in large amount boiling water, cook noodles 7 to 9 minutes until tender. Drain; return to saucepan and toss with butter.

2. Meanwhile, in medium bowl, stir together **Soup, Liquid** and **Cheese.** Stir into buttered noodles. Over medium heat, heat through, stirring constantly. Turn into serving dish; sprinkle with **Garnish.** Makes about 5 cups, 8 servings.

Spanish Rice

Meat
½ cup chopped onion
Vegetable

1 clove garlic, minced
1 cup regular rice, uncooked
1 can (10¾ to 11 ounces) condensed
Soup

1 soup can water
1 cup salsa

Meat	Vegetable	Soup
5 slices bacon, diced	½ cup chopped green pepper	tomato
½ cup diced cooked ham plus 2 tablespoons vegetable oil	1 can (4 ounces) chopped green chilies, drained	tomato rice

1. In 10-inch skillet over medium heat, cook **Meat** until lightly browned. Stir in onion, **Vegetable** and garlic; cook until vegetables are tender, stirring occasionally.

2. Stir in rice; cook until rice is slightly browned, stirring often. Stir in **Soup,** water and salsa; mix well.

3. Over high heat, heat to boiling. Reduce heat to low. Cover; simmer 25 minutes, stirring occasionally. Makes 6 servings.

Mushroom Stuffing

½ cup butter or margarine
1 cup chopped celery
1 cup chopped onion

1 cup sliced mushrooms
1 can (10¾ ounces) condensed **Soup**
½ cup **Liquid**

Bread
¼ cup chopped fresh parsley
Seasoning

Soup	Liquid	Bread	Seasoning
cream of mushroom	milk	1 loaf (1 pound) white bread, cubed	2 teaspoons rubbed dried sage
cream of chicken	water	8 cups coarsely crumbled corn bread	1 teaspoon dried thyme leaves, crushed
cream of celery	apple juice	1 loaf (1 pound) raisin bread, cubed	1 teaspoon curry powder
creamy chicken mushroom	chicken broth	1 loaf (1 pound) whole wheat bread, cubed	1 teaspoon dried tarragon leaves, crushed

1. Grease 2-quart casserole. In 10-inch skillet over medium heat, in hot butter, cook celery, onion and mushrooms until vegetables are tender, stirring often. Remove from heat. Stir in **Soup** and **Liquid;** mix well.

2. In large bowl, combine **Bread,** parsley and **Seasoning.** Pour vegetable mixture over bread; toss to mix well. Turn into prepared casserole.

3. Bake at 350°F. 45 minutes or until golden. Makes 8 servings.

Spanish Rice

Salads and Sauces

⚜

Marinated Garden Salad

1 can (10¾ ounces) condensed chicken broth
⅓ cup red wine vinegar

Herb
¼ teaspoon pepper
Vegetable 1
Vegetable 2

1 medium green pepper, cut into strips
1 medium onion, sliced
Lettuce

Herb	Vegetable 1	Vegetable 2
½ teaspoon dried basil leaves, crushed	3 medium zucchini, thinly sliced	2 medium tomatoes, cut into wedges
2 tablespoons chopped fresh chives	2 medium cucumbers, thinly sliced	2 cups carrots cut into julienne strips
½ teaspoon dried tarragon leaves, crushed	½ pound snow peas	1 can (7 ounces) sliced water chestnuts, drained
½ teaspoon rubbed dried sage	½ pound small whole mushrooms	2 cups drained, cooked cut green beans

1. In large bowl, combine chicken broth, vinegar, **Herb** and pepper; mix well.

2. Add **Vegetable 1, Vegetable 2,** green pepper and onion; toss gently to mix. Cover; refrigerate until serving time, at least 4 hours, stirring occasionally. Spoon into lettuce-lined bowls. Makes about 4 cups, 6 servings.

Buffet Layered Salad

1 can (10¾ ounces) condensed **Soup**
1 cup **Base**
¼ cup grated Parmesan cheese

1 tablespoon grated onion
6 cups torn salad greens
2 medium **Vegetables,** thinly sliced
2 cups sliced mushrooms

2 medium tomatoes, diced
½ cup chopped green onions
Garnish

Soup	Base	Vegetables	Garnish
cream of mushroom	sour cream	carrots	sliced pitted ripe olives
cream of celery	plain yogurt	zucchini	chopped fresh parsley
cream of chicken	mayonnaise	cucumbers	chopped hard-cooked egg

1. To make dressing: In medium bowl, combine **Soup, Base,** cheese and onion. Mix until smooth; set aside.

2. In clear 4-quart bowl, layer salad greens, **Vegetables,** mushrooms and tomatoes. Spoon dressing over salad, spreading to cover salad. Cover; refrigerate until serving time, at least 4 hours.

3. Sprinkle with green onions and **Garnish** before serving. Makes 12 servings.

Tip: *Use your favorite salad greens; choose from iceberg, Boston, Bibb and leaf lettuce, as well as spinach, arugula, radicchio and watercress.*

Marinated Garden Salad

Blue Ribbon Carrot Salad

2 pounds carrots, cut into 2- by
¼-inch sticks
1 can (10¾ ounces) condensed
tomato soup

¼ cup sugar
½ cup vinegar
¼ cup vegetable oil

1 teaspoon **Seasoning**
1 teaspoon Worcestershire
Vegetable 1
Vegetable 2

Seasoning	Vegetable 1	Vegetable 2
prepared mustard	1 cup sliced celery	1 cup fresh snow peas, halved crosswise, cooked and drained
dry mustard	1 medium onion, sliced	1 green pepper, cut into strips
prepared horseradish	½ cup sliced radishes	1 cup drained, cooked cut green beans
chili powder	½ cup sliced green onions	1 medium cucumber, halved lengthwise and sliced

1. In 4-quart saucepan over medium heat, in 1 inch boiling water, cook carrots until tender. Drain; cool slightly.

2. In large bowl, combine soup, sugar, vinegar, oil, **Seasoning** and Worcestershire.

3. Add cooked carrots, **Vegetable 1** and **Vegetable 2;** toss to coat well. Cover; refrigerate until serving time, at least 4 hours. Makes about 6 cups, 8 servings.

To Microwave: In 2-quart microwave-safe casserole, combine carrots and ¼ cup water; cover. Microwave on HIGH 8 to 12 minutes until tender, stirring twice. Let stand, covered, 2 minutes. Drain; cool slightly. Proceed as in Steps 2 and 3.

Tip: *The dressing on this salad also makes a delicious marinade for broiled or grilled meats.*

Creamy Coleslaw

1 can (10¾ ounces) condensed **Soup**
½ cup mayonnaise

¼ cup vinegar
½ teaspoon **Seasoning**
8 cups shredded cabbage

Vegetable
¼ cup finely chopped onion

Soup	Seasoning	Vegetable
cream of celery	caraway seed	½ cup chopped green pepper
cream of chicken	dried tarragon leaves, crushed	½ cup shredded carrot
cream of mushroom	celery seed	2 tablespoons chopped pimento

1. In large bowl, combine **Soup,** mayonnaise, vinegar and **Seasoning;** stir until smooth.

2. Add remaining ingredients; toss gently to mix well. Cover; refrigerate until serving time, at least 4 hours. Makes about 6 cups, 8 servings.

Blue Ribbon Carrot Salad

German-Style Potato Salad

2 pounds small new potatoes
2 hard-cooked eggs, sliced
Seasoning
Meat

½ cup chopped onion
2 tablespoons vegetable oil
2 tablespoons all-purpose flour
2 tablespoons sugar
⅓ cup cider vinegar

1 can (10¾ ounces) condensed
chicken broth
⅓ cup water
Dash pepper
Garnish

Seasoning	Meat	Garnish
½ teaspoon dried dill weed, crushed	½ pound kielbasa, diced	sliced pimento-stuffed olives
2 tablespoons chopped fresh parsley	6 slices bacon, diced (omit oil)	chopped green onions
¼ cup shredded carrot	½ cup diced cooked ham	chopped green pepper
½ teaspoon celery seed	4 frankfurters, sliced	diced pimento

1. In 4-quart saucepan, place potatoes; add water to cover. Over high heat, heat to boiling. Reduce heat to low; cover. Simmer 20 to 30 minutes until fork-tender; drain. Cool slightly; cut potatoes into slices.

2. In large bowl, combine potatoes, eggs and **Seasoning;** set aside.

3. In 10-inch skillet over medium heat, cook **Meat** and onion in hot oil until meat is well browned, stirring occasion-ally. (Omit oil for bacon.) Remove meat and onion with slotted spoon; add to potato mixture. Reserve drippings in skillet.

4. Stir flour into drippings. Cook 1 minute, stirring constantly. Add sugar, vinegar, broth, water and pepper. Cook until mixture boils, stirring constantly. Pour over potato mixture; toss gently to mix well. Sprinkle with **Garnish.** Serve warm. Makes about 6 cups, 8 servings.

Potato Salad

3 pounds potatoes
1 can (10¾ ounces) condensed **Soup**
¾ cup mayonnaise

2 tablespoons red wine vinegar
Seasoning
1 cup chopped celery

Vegetable 1
½ cup **Vegetable 2**
2 hard-cooked eggs, chopped

Soup	Seasoning	Vegetable 1	Vegetable 2
cream of celery	⅛ teaspoon pepper	¾ cup drained, cooked peas	sliced radishes
cream of chicken	¼ teaspoon dry mustard	¼ cup chopped green onions	chopped cucumber
cream of mushroom	⅛ teaspoon ground red pepper	½ cup diced zucchini	sliced pitted ripe olives

1. In 4-quart saucepan, place potatoes; add water to cover. Over high heat, heat to boiling. Reduce heat to low; cover. Simmer 20 to 30 minutes until fork-tender; drain. Cool slightly. Peel potatoes; cut potatoes into ½-inch cubes.

2. In large bowl, mix together **Soup,** mayonnaise, vinegar and **Seasoning** until well blended.

3. Add potatoes, celery, **Vegetable 1, Vegetable 2** and eggs; toss gently to mix. Cover; refrigerate until serving time, at least 4 hours. Makes about 7 cups, 8 servings.

German-Style Potato Salad

Fruited Salad Mold

Fruit	1 can (10¾ ounces) condensed cream of celery soup	**Dairy**
2 tablespoons sugar		½ cup **Addition**
2 envelopes unflavored gelatin	1 container (8 ounces) creamed cottage cheese	Fresh fruit and celery leaves

Fruit	Dairy	Addition
2 packages (10 ounces each) frozen raspberries, thawed	1½ cups sour cream	chopped celery
1 can (20 ounces) crushed pineapple	1 cup heavy cream, whipped	chopped walnuts
1 can (16 ounces) sliced peaches, cut up	1½ cups plain yogurt	chopped apple
1 can (16 ounces) sliced pears, cut up	1 carton (8 ounces) frozen whipped dessert topping, thawed	shredded carrot

1. Drain **Fruit,** reserving liquid. Measure liquid; add enough water to make 1 cup liquid, if necessary. Pour liquid into 1-quart saucepan; add sugar. Sprinkle gelatin over liquid. Let stand 5 minutes. Over low heat, heat until gelatin is dissolved, stirring constantly. Pour into large bowl.

2. Stir in drained fruit and soup. Refrigerate 1 to 1½ hours until almost set.

3. Fold in cottage cheese, **Dairy** and **Addition.** Pour into 7-cup mold. Refrigerate until set, at least 4 hours or overnight.

4. Unmold onto serving platter. Garnish with fresh fruit and celery leaves. Makes 8 servings.

Rice Salad

1 can (10¾ ounces) condensed chicken broth	1 cup regular rice, uncooked	1 cup chopped celery
¾ cup water	½ cup mayonnaise	**Addition 1**
	½ cup sour cream	**Addition 2**
	Liquid	

Liquid	Addition 1	Addition 2
½ cup pineapple juice	1⅓ cups halved seedless grapes	2 medium bananas, sliced
⅓ cup orange juice plus 3 tablespoons lemon juice	½ cup sliced green onions	2 hard-cooked eggs, chopped
⅓ cup apple juice plus 2 tablespoons vinegar	½ cup green pepper strips	1½ cups halved cherry tomatoes

1. In 2-quart saucepan over high heat, heat broth and water to boiling. Stir in rice. Reduce heat to low. Cover; simmer 20 minutes or until tender. Remove from heat.

2. In large bowl, combine mayonnaise, sour cream and **Liquid;** mix until blended. Stir in rice, celery and **Addition 1.** Cover; refrigerate until serving time, at least 4 hours.

3. Just before serving, stir in **Addition 2.** Makes about 5 cups, 6 servings.

Fruited Salad Mold

Tomato French Dressing

1 can (10¾ ounces) condensed tomato soup

½ cup vegetable oil
¼ cup **Liquid**

Seasoning
Flavoring

Liquid	Seasoning	Flavoring
cider vinegar	½ teaspoon dry mustard	4 slices bacon, cooked, drained and crumbled
lemon juice	1 tablespoon grated onion	¼ cup crumbled blue cheese
wine vinegar	1 tablespoon finely chopped green onion	1 clove garlic, minced

1. In covered jar or shaker, combine all ingredients; shake well before using.

2. Serve over mixed salad greens or fruit salads. Makes about 2 cups.

Low-Calorie Salad Dressing

1 can (10¾ ounces) condensed chicken broth
⅓ cup vinegar

2 tablespoons vegetable oil
Generous dash pepper

Addition
Flavoring 1
Flavoring 2

Addition	Flavoring 1	Flavoring 2
¼ cup finely chopped tomato	1 tablespoon chopped fresh parsley	1 clove garlic, minced
1 tablespoon toasted sesame seed	1 teaspoon grated lemon peel	few drops hot pepper sauce
2 tablespoons finely chopped green onion	1 teaspoon dried tarragon leaves, crushed	2 teaspoons Dijon-style mustard

In covered jar or shaker, combine all ingredients; shake well before using. Serve over salad greens. Makes about 2 cups.

Tomato-Cucumber Dressing

1 can (10¾ ounces) condensed **Soup**
1 cup **Base**
1 cup chopped tomato, drained

½ cup chopped seeded cucumber
Herb

1 tablespoon grated onion
⅛ teaspoon pepper
½ cup milk

Soup	Base	Herb
cream of mushroom	plain yogurt	¼ cup chopped fresh parsley plus 1 teaspoon chopped fresh dill
cream of celery	mayonnaise	2 tablespoons chopped fresh chives
cream of chicken	sour cream	2 tablespoons chopped fresh basil leaves

In medium bowl, combine **Soup** and **Base,** stirring until well blended. Add remaining ingredients; mix well. Refrigerate until serving time, at least 4 hours. Serve over mixed salad greens. Makes about 3 cups.

Golden Mushroom Sauce

2 tablespoons butter or margarine
Vegetable

1 can (10¾ ounces) condensed
golden mushroom soup

Liquid
Seasoning

Vegetable	Liquid	Seasoning
2 tablespoons chopped shallots	⅓ cup water plus ¼ cup dry red wine	1 tablespoon chopped fresh parsley
¼ cup chopped onion	⅓ cup water plus ¼ cup dry sherry	⅛ teaspoon dried thyme leaves, crushed
⅓ cup chopped green pepper	½ cup milk	1 tablespoon chopped fresh chives

1. In 2-quart saucepan over medium heat, in hot butter, cook **Vegetable** until tender, stirring occasionally.

2. Stir in soup, **Liquid** and **Seasoning;** heat until boiling, stirring frequently. Serve over beef, lamb or meat loaf. Makes about 2 cups.

To Microwave: In 1-quart microwave-safe casserole, combine butter and **Vegetable;** cover. Microwave on HIGH 1 to 2 minutes until vegetable is tender. Stir in soup, **Liquid** and **Seasoning.** Microwave, uncovered, on HIGH 3 to 5 minutes until boiling, stirring once.

Homemade Gravy

Drippings from roast meat or poultry
1 can (10½ to 10¾ ounces)
condensed **Soup**

½ soup can water
2 tablespoons cornstarch

Seasoning 1
Seasoning 2

Soup	Seasoning 1	Seasoning 2
French onion	¼ teaspoon dried thyme leaves, crushed	1 teaspoon Worcestershire
chicken broth	1 teaspoon soy sauce	⅛ teaspoon ground ginger
golden mushroom (omit cornstarch)	½ teaspoon dried basil leaves, crushed	dash ground red pepper

Remove meat or poultry from pan. Pour off pan drippings, reserving 2 tablespoons in pan. Pour **Soup** into roasting pan; stir well to loosen brown bits. In small bowl, stir together water and cornstarch; stir into roasting pan along with **Seasoning 1** and **Seasoning 2**. (Omit cornstarch for golden mushroom soup.) Over medium heat, heat to boiling, stirring constantly; cook 1 minute more. Serve with meat or poultry. Makes about 2 cups.

Fruited Barbecue Sauce

2 tablespoons vegetable oil
½ cup chopped onion
1 clove garlic, minced

1 can (10½ to 10¾ ounces)
condensed **Soup**

1 cup **Preserves**
¼ cup **Liquid**
1 tablespoon soy sauce

Soup	Preserves	Liquid
beef broth	apricot preserves	lemon juice
chicken broth	peach preserves	cider vinegar
French onion	orange marmalade	lime juice

In 2-quart saucepan over medium heat, in hot oil, cook onion and garlic until tender, stirring occasionally. Stir in remaining ingredients. Reduce heat to low; simmer, uncovered, 15 minutes, stirring occasionally. Use to baste chicken or ribs during last 15 minutes of barbecuing. Heat remaining sauce; spoon over meat. Makes about 2 cups.

Blender Hollandaise Sauce

1 can (10¾ ounces) condensed **Soup**
3 egg yolks

2 tablespoons lemon juice
⅛ teaspoon **Seasoning 1**

Dash **Seasoning 2**
½ cup butter or margarine, melted

Soup	Seasoning 1	Seasoning 2
cream of asparagus	hot pepper sauce	freshly ground pepper
cream of chicken	dry mustard	lemon-pepper seasoning
cream of celery	grated lemon peel	ground red pepper

1. In blender or food processor, combine **Soup,** egg yolks, lemon juice, **Seasoning 1** and **Seasoning 2.** Cover; blend or process until smooth.

2. At high speed, very slowly add butter in a steady stream; blend or process 3 minutes more or until thickened. Pour into 1½-quart saucepan. Over low heat, heat through, stirring often. Do not boil. Serve over vegetables, eggs or fish. Makes about 2 cups.

Souper Cream Sauce

1 can (10¾ to 11 ounces) condensed **Soup**

½ cup **Liquid**

Flavoring
Seasoning

Soup	Liquid	Flavoring	Seasoning
cream of celery	half-and-half	1 tablespoon prepared mustard	⅛ teaspoon paprika
Cheddar cheese	milk	2 slices bacon, cooked, drained and crumbled	½ cup shredded Cheddar cheese
cream of chicken	sour cream	1 tablespoon chopped fresh chives	1 teaspoon grated lemon peel

In 2-quart saucepan, combine all ingredients. Over medium heat, heat through, stirring often. Serve over vegetables, meat or fish. Makes about 1½ cups.

Sour Cream Sauce

2 tablespoons butter or margarine
Vegetable

Seasoning
1 can (10¾ ounces) condensed **Soup**

⅓ cup sour cream
⅓ cup milk

Vegetable	Seasoning	Soup
½ cup sliced mushrooms	1 teaspoon Worcestershire	cream of mushroom
⅓ cup chopped onion	¼ teaspoon paprika	golden mushroom
½ cup chopped celery	¼ teaspoon curry powder	cream of celery
½ cup shredded carrot	¼ teaspoon dried tarragon leaves, crushed	creamy chicken mushroom

In 2-quart saucepan over medium heat, in hot butter, cook **Vegetable** and **Seasoning** until vegetable is tender, stirring occasionally. Stir in **Soup,** sour cream and milk. Heat through, stirring occasionally. Thin to desired consistency with additional milk, if desired. Serve over meat, vegetables, pasta or rice. Makes about 2 cups.

Blender Hollandaise Sauce

Breads and Desserts

❦

Giant Zucchini Muffins

2½ cups all-purpose flour
Addition
⅓ cup sugar
1 tablespoon baking powder

Dried **Herb,** crushed
1 can (10¾ to 11 ounces) condensed
Soup
½ cup **Liquid**

2 eggs
¼ cup vegetable oil
1 cup shredded zucchini

Addition	Herb	Soup	Liquid
1 cup cornmeal	1 teaspoon oregano leaves	nacho cheese	milk
½ cup wheat germ	1 teaspoon summer savory leaves	cream of celery	orange juice
½ cup finely chopped nuts	½ teaspoon thyme leaves	cream of mushroom	water

1. Preheat oven to 400°F. Grease twelve 3-inch muffin-pan cups. In large bowl, combine flour, **Addition,** sugar, baking powder and **Herb.** In medium bowl, combine **Soup, Liquid,** eggs, oil and zucchini; mix well. Add to dry ingredients, stirring to moisten. (Batter will be lumpy.)

2. Spoon batter into muffin cups, filling almost full. Bake 25 minutes or until toothpick inserted in center of muffin comes out clean. Serve warm. Makes 12 muffins.

Double Cheese Ring

Flour
2 tablespoons sugar
4 teaspoons baking powder
¾ cup shortening

1 can (11 ounces) condensed Cheddar
cheese soup/sauce
¼ cup milk
4 ounces **Cheese,** thinly sliced

1 egg yolk
2 teaspoons water
Topping

Flour	Cheese	Topping
1 cup whole wheat plus 2 cups all-purpose	American	poppy seed
3 cups all-purpose	Cheddar	sesame seed
½ cup rye plus 2½ cups all-purpose	Swiss	caraway seed
½ cup wheat germ plus 2½ cups all-purpose	Monterey Jack	minced dried onion

1. Preheat oven to 425°F. Grease large baking sheet. In large bowl, stir together **Flour,** sugar and baking powder. With pastry blender, cut in shortening until mixture resembles coarse crumbs.

2. In small bowl, combine soup and milk; mix well. Add to flour mixture, stirring with fork just until dough forms. Turn out onto lightly floured surface. Knead dough 10 times. Divide dough in half.

3. Roll out each dough half to 12-inch circle. Cut each into 8 wedges. Cut sliced **Cheese** into sixteen 3- by ½-inch strips. Place 1 piece cheese on each wedge. Roll up jelly-roll fashion from outside edge. On prepared baking sheet, arrange rolls side-by-side to form a ring.

4. In small bowl, combine egg yolk and water; brush on ring. Sprinkle with **Topping.** Bake 25 to 30 minutes until browned. Serve warm. Makes 16 servings.

Giant Zucchini Muffins

German Cheese Fruit Kuchen

3½ to 3¾ cups all-purpose flour,
divided

¼ cup sugar

2 packages active dry yeast

1 can (11 ounces) condensed Cheddar
cheese soup/sauce, divided

½ cup water

¼ cup butter or margarine

4 eggs, divided

Filling

1 package (8 ounces) cream cheese,
softened

⅓ cup sugar

Flavoring 1

Flavoring 2

Topping

Filling	Flavoring 1	Flavoring 2	Topping
1 can (21 ounces) cherry pie filling	1 tablespoon grated orange peel	2 tablespoons orange juice	ground nutmeg
4 cups shredded apples tossed with ¼ cup additional sugar	2 teaspoons grated lemon peel	2 tablespoons lemon juice	vanilla wafer crumbs
1 can (21 ounces) blueberry pie filling	2 teaspoons vanilla extract	1 teaspoon ground cinnamon	gingersnap crumbs
1 can (20 ounces) crushed pineapple, drained	¼ teaspoon almond extract	2 tablespoons orange liqueur	toasted flaked coconut

1. In large bowl, stir together 1½ cups of the flour, ¼ cup sugar and yeast. In 1-quart saucepan over low heat, heat ½ cup of the soup, water and butter until mixture is very warm (120° to 130°F.). Butter does not need to melt completely.

2. With mixer at low speed, gradually pour soup mixture into dry ingredients. At medium speed, beat 2 minutes, scraping bowl with rubber spatula. Beat in 2 of the eggs and ½ cup of the flour; beat 2 minutes more, scraping bowl occasionally.

3. With spoon, stir in enough additional flour (about 1½ cups) to make a soft dough. On floured surface, knead until smooth and elastic, about 5 minutes.

4. Shape dough into ball; place in greased large bowl, turning dough to grease top. Cover; let rise in warm place until doubled, about 45 minutes.

5. Grease 13- by 9-inch baking pan. Press dough into prepared pan, making 1-inch rim on edges. Top with **Filling.** Cover and let rise until doubled, about 30 minutes. Preheat oven to 350°F.

6. Meanwhile, in small bowl with mixer at medium speed, beat cream cheese and remaining soup until smooth. Beat in remaining 2 eggs and ⅓ cup sugar. Stir in **Flavoring 1** and **Flavoring 2;** pour over filling. Sprinkle with **Topping.**

7. Bake 45 to 55 minutes until crust is golden brown and cheese is set. Cool slightly in pan on rack. Serve warm. Makes 12 servings.

Tip: *Yeast bread recipes often specify a range for the amount of flour. This range is necessary because the moistness of yeast dough can vary from day to day. The moistness depends on the weather, the temperature of the other ingredients, the amount of liquid and the cook's kneading technique.*

On humid days, you will probably need the greater amount of flour, perhaps even more than stated in the recipe. You'll also need more flour if the yeast mixture is at a higher temperature or if you're using extra-large eggs.

How do you know how much flour to use? Start by using the low end of the range, then add more if the dough is still sticky. Remember, the flour you add during kneading counts as part of the total amount. When your dough has enough flour, it will have a smooth nonsticky surface that will spring back when you touch it.

Be sure to have enough flour in the dough before it rises. If you add flour after the dough starts rising, the bread will have dark streaks and a coarse texture.

Fruited Spice Cake Squares

1 package (2-layer size) spice cake mix
1 can (10¾ ounces) condensed tomato soup

½ cup water
2 eggs
1 cup **Fruit**
½ cup butter or margarine, softened

3 cups confectioners' sugar
1 teaspoon **Flavoring**
3 tablespoons **Liquid**
1 cup **Topping**

Fruit	Flavoring	Liquid	Topping
raisins	grated orange peel	orange juice	finely chopped walnuts
chopped dried apricots	vanilla extract	milk	granola
chopped prunes	grated lemon peel	apple juice	toasted flaked coconut

1. Preheat oven to 350°F. Grease 15- by 10-inch jelly-roll pan; set aside.

2. In medium bowl, mix cake mix, tomato soup, water and eggs, following directions on package. Fold in **Fruit.** Pour batter into prepared pan.

3. Bake 25 to 30 minutes until toothpick inserted in cake comes out clean. Cool completely in pan on wire rack.

4. In medium bowl, beat butter until creamy. Gradually add confectioners' sugar, **Flavoring** and **Liquid,** stirring until smooth. Spread on cake; sprinkle with **Topping.** Cut cake into squares. Makes 24 squares.

Tip: *This cake can be baked in two greased 9- by 5-inch loaf pans at 350°F. 45 minutes. Cool in pans 10 minutes, then cool completely on wire racks before frosting. Slice to serve.*

Three-Fruit Cake Squares

2 cups all-purpose flour
1 teaspoon baking powder
½ teaspoon baking soda
Ground **Spice**

½ cup butter or margarine
1½ cups sugar
2 eggs
1 can (10¾ ounces) condensed tomato soup

Flavoring
½ cup chopped apple
½ cup **Fruit**
½ cup **Dried Fruit**
Confectioners' sugar

Spice	Flavoring	Fruit	Dried Fruit
1 teaspoon nutmeg	1 teaspoon grated lemon peel	chopped fresh or frozen cranberries	chopped dried apricots
1 teaspoon cinnamon	½ teaspoon almond extract	drained crushed pineapple	raisins
½ teaspoon allspice plus ½ teaspoon ginger	1 teaspoon vanilla extract	fresh or frozen blueberries	chopped dried figs

1. Preheat oven to 350°F. Grease and flour 13- by 9-inch baking pan.

2. In medium bowl, stir together flour, baking powder, baking soda and **Spice;** set aside.

3. In large bowl with mixer at medium speed, cream together butter and sugar until light and fluffy. Beat in eggs, one at a time, beating well after each addition. Add soup and **Flavoring** alternately with flour mixture, beating 1 minute after each addition.

4. Stir in apple, **Fruit** and **Dried Fruit** just until mixed. Pour into prepared pan. Bake 40 minutes or until toothpick inserted in cake comes out clean. Cool in pan on wire rack. Dust with confectioners' sugar. Makes 15 servings.

Mini Cheddar Cheesecakes

⅔ cup **Crumbs**
12 ounces cream cheese, softened
1 can (11 ounces) condensed Cheddar
cheese soup/sauce

¾ cup sugar
3 eggs
Flavoring 1

Flavoring 2
1 teaspoon vanilla extract
Topping

Crumbs	Flavoring 1	Flavoring 2	Topping
graham cracker	1 teaspoon grated lime peel	2 tablespoons lime juice	sour cream and fresh fruit
cinnamon graham cracker	½ teaspoon almond extract	½ cup chopped pistachios	canned cherry pie filling
vanilla wafer	1 teaspoon grated lemon peel	2 tablespoons lemon juice	whipped cream and ground nutmeg
chocolate wafer	¼ cup unsweetened cocoa	1 tablespoon crème de cacao or coffee liqueur	coffee-flavored yogurt and chocolate curls

1. Line 16 muffin-pan cups with foil or paper cupcake liners. Spoon about 1½ teaspoons **Crumbs** into each; set aside. Preheat oven to 325°F.

2. In large bowl with mixer at medium speed, beat together cream cheese, soup, sugar, eggs, **Flavoring 1, Flavoring 2** and vanilla until smooth and creamy. Spoon batter into prepared muffin cups.

3. Bake 35 minutes or until set (cheesecakes will sink in centers). Cool in pan on wire rack. Cover; refrigerate until serving time, at least 2 hours.

4. Decorate with **Topping.** Makes 16 mini cheesecakes.

Spicy Vegetable Cake

2 cups all-purpose flour
1⅓ cups packed brown sugar
2 teaspoons baking powder
1 teaspoon baking soda

Ground **Spice**
1 can (10¾ ounces) condensed
tomato soup
½ cup shortening

2 eggs
¼ cup **Syrup**
1 cup shredded **Vegetable**
½ cup **Addition**

Spice	Syrup	Vegetable	Addition
1 teaspoon allspice plus 1 teaspoon nutmeg plus 1 teaspoon cinnamon	molasses	carrots	raisins
1½ teaspoons ginger plus ½ teaspoon cloves plus ½ teaspoon cinnamon	honey	zucchini	flaked coconut
1 tablespoon pumpkin pie spice	maple-flavored syrup	peeled sweet potatoes	chopped nuts

1. Preheat oven to 350°F. Grease 10-inch tube pan.

2. In large bowl, combine flour, brown sugar, baking powder, baking soda and **Spice.** Add soup and shortening. With mixer at medium speed, beat 2 minutes, constantly scraping sides and bottom of bowl.

3. Add eggs and **Syrup;** beat 2 minutes more. Fold in **Vegetable** and **Addition.** Turn into prepared pan; bake about 1 hour or until toothpick inserted in cake comes out clean. Cool in pan on wire rack 10 minutes. Remove from pan; cool completely. Serve plain or topped with whipped cream. Makes 16 servings.

Tip: *You can bake this cake in a greased and floured 13- by 9-inch baking pan at 350°F. 40 to 50 minutes. Or, bake in 2 greased and floured 9-inch round cake pans at 350°F. 30 to 35 minutes. Layer cooled cakes with whipped cream.*

Mini Cheddar Cheesecakes

Index